Magic Symbols
of the World

Magic
of the

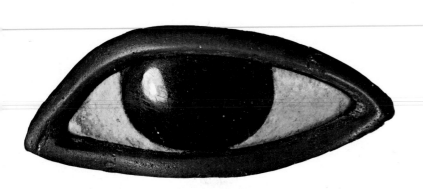

Magic's 'fundamental conception is
identical with that of modern science;
underlying the whole system is a faith,
implicit but real and firm, in the
order and uniformity of nature.'

Sir James Frazer *The Golden Bough*

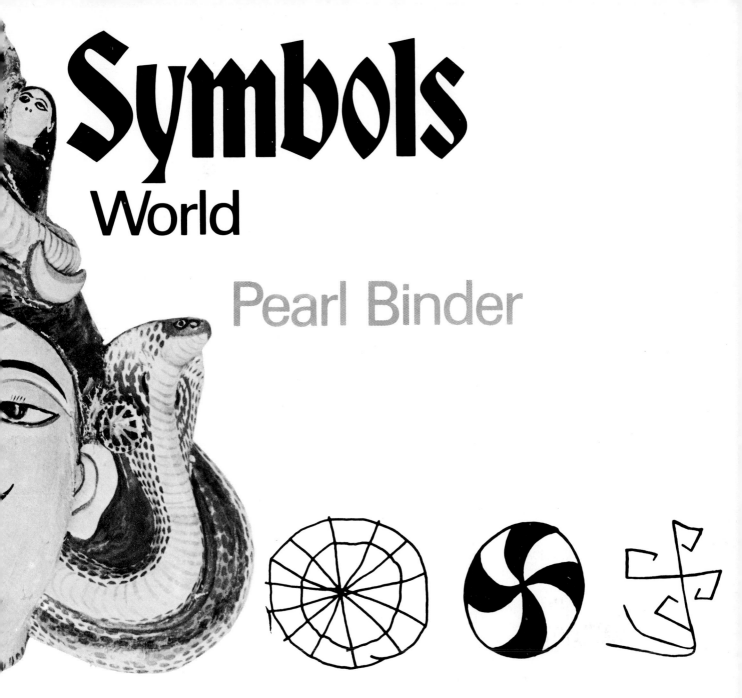

Symbols
World

Pearl Binder

Hamlyn
London · New York · Sydney · Toronto

To my daughter Elizabeth

Published by
THE HAMLYN PUBLISHING GROUP LIMITED
London · New York · Sydney · Toronto
Hamlyn House, Feltham, Middlesex, England

ISBN 0 600 02545 4

Filmsetting in England by Filmtype Services Limited, Scarborough
Printed in Spain by Printer, Industria Gráfica S. A.
Tuset 19, Barcelona, San Vicente dels Horts 1972
Depósito Legal B. 24204-1972
Mohn Gordon Ltd., London
Text set in 11/12 pt Monophoto Plantin 110
Captions set in 8/9 pt Univers Medium

Contents

6   What is magic?

18   Symbols of fertility

30   Gods as symbols

50   Magic protection of body and dwelling

72   Magic protection of family and livelihood

100   Death and after-life

116   Conclusion

124   Acknowledgments

126   Index

Even without man's inhumanity to man, the natural calamities of flood, drought, earthquake, volcano, locust, and epidemic cause millions of helpless people suffering—and many death. When war and conquest are added the toll on millions of refugees becomes unbearable: torn from their homes, in panic and fear, their family life destroyed, their few possessions abandoned. It is people like these, whose everyday life is hazardous, who turn to magic for security and protection.

What is magic?

The need for security

This book is about magic communication by images and symbols, the oldest and most popular forms of communication.

You who are reading this book belong to the world of modern technology. You can read. You can obtain water by turning on a tap, a doctor by a telephone call, food and drink from a well-supplied store within reasonable reach. You can avoid the cold of winter by central heating and the heat of summer by air conditioning. You fear neither starvation nor savage beast. You have banished darkness from your home and you do not live in terror of sorcery.

But you are privileged. Almost all people in even the recent past could not read. They lived precariously, their meagre crops threatened by pest, earthquake, drought and flood, and their lives undermined by pestilence and fear of witchcraft. Their life expectation was brief and most of their children died young.

It is not surprising, therefore, that their constant preoccupation was with security and continuity. They wanted their crops to grow and their children to survive. In their eyes everything that protected life was good and everything that threatened life was bad. They believed the universe to be orderly but menaced by destructive demons bent on disturbing the order and promoting chaos, disease and death. To protect themselves, their livestock and crops from these destructive demons, they created deities of life-giving power. They believed these gods were on their side, if they could only get through to them, make contact with them, explain their needs and enlist their help. And to this end they evolved ritual prayers, offerings and sacrifice.

The magic power that supports the sun in the sky, the magic power that causes the moon to wax and wane, the magic power that sends rain to swell the seeds, the magic power that multiplies the game and the magic power that enables man to procreate, all these are the magic powers of nature. This total magic power, in all its endless manifestations, had to be invoked, coaxed and propitiated in the manner believed to be most pleasing to the gods. No one got something for nothing. Favours had to be paid for. Gods were a human conception and therefore it was believed that they would enjoy what human beings enjoy, that is food, drink, jewels, beautiful clothes, music and dancing, flattery, and painful sacrifices to impress their worshippers' need.

On such worship and sacrifice to the mighty forces of nature, all religions and all civilizations have been based. Scientific progress in the modern world has now given us computers, Jumbo jets, organ transplants, food preservatives and atomic power. But the scientist in his costly modern laboratory is still seeking – no less avidly than the primitive bushman hopefully fumbling pebbles into lucky patterns – to contain the whirlwind, to prolong human life and above all to foretell the future.

In many countries of the world today modern technology is still absent or unavailable to most of the inhabitants. Robert MacNamara, President of the World Bank, gave the following statistics on 21 September 1970: between one-third and one-half of the world's people suffer from hunger or nutritional deprivation; infant deaths per thousand live births are four times as high in the developing countries as in the developed countries; there are 100,000,000 more illiterates today than there were twenty years ago; and approximately 20 per cent of the entire male labour force in the world is unemployed. 'Developing countries' means countries like India, Africa, the Arab states, South America, and some of the islands in the Pacific, Atlantic and Indian oceans.

It is in countries like these, where food is scarce, medical help a luxury if obtainable at all, and poverty endemic, that poor people turn to magic for comfort and hope. They need and seek good luck; they need continual personal reassurance, and over thousands of years have evolved their own patterns and symbols of security and protection. Their dwellings, clothes, animals, children and jobs are heavily guarded by magic patterns and symbols. For the right pattern will keep out the bad spirits, and also, by repetition, provide reassurance that life is going to continue. Illiterate peoples use symbols instead of writing and hope, by constant use of such symbols, to comfort themselves and remind the gods to help them.

The fact that today many people in the affluent nations are turning towards magic is proof that they too feel insecure.

Symbols are direct

In order to understand popular symbols we must first try to understand how ordinary, uneducated people think and feel. Ordinary people do not understand the subtle reasoning of scholarship, nor are they attracted to abstract ideology. They are ruled by their emotions and by their domestic loyalties. They need to see and touch in order to understand, and they understand in a personal way. Above all they believe deeply in life, and they need images and symbols to reassure them, by magic power, that life will triumph over its enemies. Once ordinary people have established an emotional relationship with a symbol, they remain absolutely steadfast to their choice, and their loyalty is unshakeable. Over thousands of years of different régimes and different rulers, each bringing strange new images and alien symbols, the common people will continue (when necessary in secret, and sometimes without even knowing why) to worship their chosen images of magic power.

The scholar's academic approach to the origin of popular images and symbols has no meaning for those very people who most use them. Our museums are filled with extraordinary images of the past, whose history we who can read are grateful to learn from the patient research of learned scholars. But not everyone is literate. There is no doubt that the masses of uneducated people do not regard images and symbols in the same way as the scholars. There are in fact two languages of understanding. The understanding of the uneducated is direct, concrete, timeless and highly practical. Let us take one example, the matter of the Buddha's ear-lobes.

Remarkable in all images of the Buddha are the extremely large ears. Some authorities explain this phenomenon by the fact that the Buddha, a prince in real life, would have worn the heavy ear-ornaments of his rank which, by their weight, would have distended his ear-lobes. Therefore, they argue, the large ears are symbolic of his noble birth. But this is not what millions of devout Asian peasants believe. To them he is more than a prince: he is a god with godly powers. They believe, because they need to believe, that Buddha has large ears in order that he can receive the endless prayers for help poured into them unceasingly. To his peasant worshippers Buddha is not the classic disinterested deity intent only on his own enlightenment, but the magic lord of mercy and kindness to whom they pray for succour.

So, when we are dealing with popular beliefs, it is wise to try to see the situation from below, where most people are.

The fact that the poor can afford so few distractions and are accustomed to making things for themselves gives a robust originality to their interpretation of magic symbols, a crude vitality not to be found in the formal perfection of the adornment of the privileged. All the world over the common people, like children, prefer strong colours, geometric repeated patterns, glitter and vividly optimistic definition. The imagination of unlettered people, like that of unspoiled children, is always resourceful and audacious.

Even the deadly inroads of industrialization cannot destroy the richly imaginative

Pablo Picasso once said that when art is properly understood we will be able to paint pictures to cure toothache. Witchdoctors would agree with him. In these popular paired plates, part of a series which were his gift to the exhausted people of France in the difficult years following the Second World War, Picasso symbolizes the Life/Death struggle always facing civilization. In his long working life the creator of a dazzling succession of disintegration schools of painting, Picasso constantly returns to this classic style to restate his belief in the wholeness of life. *Top*: War/Death. *Above*: Peace/Life.
Designed by Pablo Picasso. Glazed white ceramic, black line. Diameter 9 ins. 1950. Maison de la Pensée, Paris. © by S.P.A.D.E.M., Paris, 1972.

9

popular inspiration. At the time of the coronation of Elizabeth II, the decorations in the East End of London, paid for by the people who lived in those dingy streets and planned and carried out by them, were so lively and imaginative that they outshone the official street decorations of the West End.

Another reason for the directness of the symbols of common people is their belief that spirits have a lot to do and cannot be expected to sort out vague and unspecified prayers. A good example of this occurs among the peasant women of the Miao tribes of southern China, near Burma. When they are working in the fields, they wear a handsome dress which has a wide skirt with a heavy broad border intricately patterned in varying squares enclosed between bands. The embroidery of these borders takes a very long time, and Chinese Communists, anxious to get a bigger yield from these territories, offered to print the borders by machinery, so that the women could spend more time in the fields. They interviewed an old peasant woman, who explained to them the importance of these embroidered borders. She told them that the two broad bands represented the rivers which enclosed their lands. The squares represented their various fields, and the varying patterns inside the squares represented the different crops they were growing in these fields. If the patterns on the women's skirts were not absolutely precise and accurate, how would the gods know what the peasants were trying to grow, and so know how to help them? The skirt-borders were a perpetual prayer, of the most detailed and exact nature, to their deities, who could not fail to observe their visual prayer, since the women wore their skirts every day in the fields, where the help was needed.

The robes worn by the Chinese Emperor at his life-imploring rituals for the benefit of his subjects were another excellent example of the great preciseness of magic symbolism. For the worship of the moon the Emperor wore white robes; for the worship of the sun, red robes; for the worship of the earth, yellow robes; and for the worship of heaven he wore blue robes. All were richly embroidered with cosmic symbols: at the hem the wave-ridden sea and the mountains, and above the sea in a turmoil of small rain-clouds writhed a five-clawed, front-facing imperial dragon. The embroidered stripes on his robes symbolized rain; the straightness of the back seam symbolized incorruptibility and the horizontal lower-edge symbolized a clean heart and firm will: together they symbolized the perfect balance of nature. The twelve sacred emblems embroidered on his robes included stars for pardon and love, mountains for worship, the holy vessels for sacrifice, waterweed for the spirit of the waters, the imperial axe for justice, and rice grains for fertility and prosperity.

Religion and the image

Puritan religions, Judaism, Buddhism and Mohammedanism, have always struggled between their insistence on spiritual deities and the desire of the uneducated people for visual signs of these spiritual deities. Most people need to see pictures in the fire. And the theatre began in the holy temples.

The Jews renounced idolatry in favour of a single all-powerful male deity, Jehovah, who was an invisible spirit and who, in return for their unswerving devotion and moral rectitude, promised to lead them into green pastures. They were allowed to keep a few simple abstract North African patterns recalling their harsh nomad-shepherd life. These patterns the Jews interpreted as visual symbols of assurance. The black border of their white woollen garments they interpreted as God's miracle in separating light from darkness. The diamond pattern they used as the Eye of God. The pagan rayed-sun and six-pointed star they interpreted as the power of Jehovah spreading outwards from his still centre. More daring still, they believed that the three Hebrew letters which spell the divine name, most holy of holies, actually formed the very features of Jehovah himself, their invisible spirit deity. (They were the People of the Book, but almost all of them were still illiterate, and for them each letter held immense magic potency.) Their sacred Star of David, the intersected double triangle which they interpreted as symbolizing the love of man for God and God for man, is in historic fact, according to Robert Graves, an Egyptian fertility symbol of the sexual union of the pagan goddess Ashtaroth (Astarte) and Adonis.

In Cromwell's day too the most devout English Puritans practised fetishism in their fixation on the Old Testament, wearing sacred texts next to their skin under their coarse shirts.

But the object is always the same: life and the worship of life. Their symbols all symbolize life, life triumphant and life eternal, life in the next world as in this.

The Roman Catholic Church with its long history of evangelism understands the stubborn nature of symbols—that even converts cannot bear to part from their former holy symbols. So it was that in 1623 Pope Gregory XV decreed that Brahmins converted to Catholicism might continue to wear their

Polish papercut of the Tree of Life, guarded by two cocks. The reassurance of symmetry is a strong ingredient in protective magic.
Gloss paper. 10×5½ ins. Traditional; still in use. Poland. Author's collection.

sacred Brahmin cord and use their Brahmin caste marks, provided these Hindu symbols were blessed by a Roman Catholic priest. This was in the Tamil region of southern India, after twenty years of incessant missionary work by the Jesuit priest Robert de Nobili.

In creating gods and demons, human beings are giving names and shapes to their hopes and fears. In religious ritual (whether for white magic or black magic) they are trying to tap the immense forces of nature. Because sex is the most basic human urge, sex is the focus of all religions and all cults, as much repressed as released and therefore taking sinister shapes and pleasing forms.

The great Puritan religions strictly forbade the making of idols and banned imagery, in order to return to the spiritual meaning of religion. But history teaches us that symbols and imagery fulfil a deep human need and cannot be suppressed without danger. They symbolize universal forces which can be used for good or evil but cannot be ignored.

The Jews have managed to keep idols out of their religious practice. Nevertheless their ritual depends on the use of symbols. Their legends and folklore teem with angels and demons and phenomena such as spirit possession. Devout Buddhists flouted almost

at once the Buddha's strict veto on idolatry, so that today Buddhism, which has taken root in so many countries, including England, revolves round images and ritual of magic purpose. The Muslim faith (which, like Christianity, evolved from Judaism) has been fanatically strict in its veto of imagery. Devout Muslims, regarding the depiction of human, animal or plant with horror, not only totally excluded representational art from their own culture, but attacked and destroyed it in other cultures. The depiction of the human face was especially abhorrent to the Muslims, and there are defaced books and illuminations to testify to their belief. However, provided the natural shape was so highly stylized that it was not obviously a natural form and provided it was not brought inside the mosque, talismans proliferated and proliferate in all Muslim countries. Nowhere is the evil eye more believed in and more dreaded.

The original simple wooden cross of the Christian faith was soon elaborated by the faithful, so that almost every saint was awarded his own symbolic cross, and European peasants carved and embroidered flowering adorned crosses so elaborately that the cross itself was hidden. Today, three centuries after the English Puritans, the

Magic-protective symmetry in a Mexican cut-paper flag showing planets, growing plants and a repeat border including the triangular symbols of male and female sexuality (see page 87). *Brown tissue paper. 8½×6½ ins. Traditional; still in use. Mexico City. Author's collection.*

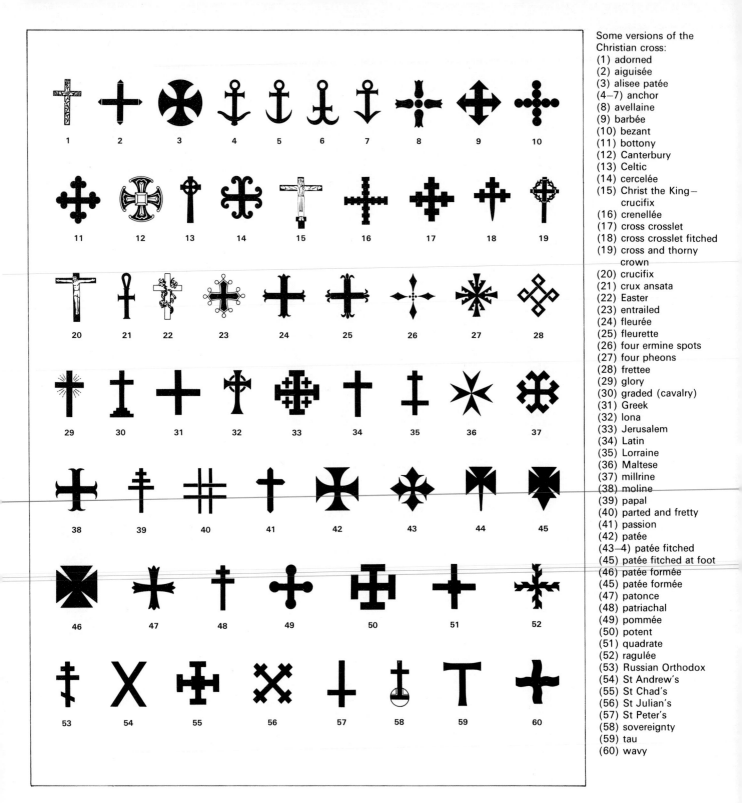

Some versions of the
Christian cross:
(1) adorned
(2) aiguisée
(3) alisee patée
(4—7) anchor
(8) avellaine
(9) barbée
(10) bezant
(11) bottony
(12) Canterbury
(13) Celtic
(14) cercelée
(15) Christ the King—
     crucifix
(16) crenellée
(17) cross crosslet
(18) cross crosslet fitched
(19) cross and thorny
     crown
(20) crucifix
(21) crux ansata
(22) Easter
(23) entrailed
(24) fleurée
(25) fleurette
(26) four ermine spots
(27) four pheons
(28) frettee
(29) glory
(30) graded (cavalry)
(31) Greek
(32) Iona
(33) Jerusalem
(34) Latin
(35) Lorraine
(36) Maltese
(37) millrine
(38) moline
(39) papal
(40) parted and fretty
(41) passion
(42) patée
(43—4) patée fitched
(45) patée fitched at foot
(46) patée formée
(45) patée formée
(47) patonce
(48) patriachal
(49) pommée
(50) potent
(51) quadrate
(52) ragulée
(53) Russian Orthodox
(54) St Andrew's
(55) St Chad's
(56) St Julian's
(57) St Peter's
(58) sovereignty
(59) tau
(60) wavy

Church of England acknowledges at least fifty different versions of the Christian cross.

It has soothed and comforted countless millions of people to be able to see visual expression of the good human qualities in the shape of gentle winged angels. It reassures them, in this harsh world, that kindness and goodness are not only abstract conceptions. Equally, it seems wiser to give concrete expression to man's dark inner emotions and searing conflicts, in the form of devils and demons, than to try unsuccessfully to repress these human terrors and become psychotic or run mad. The great religious processional festivals are lacking or rare in industrialized countries, and people feel lonely, isolated, repressed and anonymous. Our rational age of science and reason is marked by a staggering increase in psychiatric ailments. The findings of modern psychology explain to us that Satan, with goat feet, tail and horns, is merely Pan, the image of wishful thinking for the delight and danger of sex. But this understanding does not cure the patient, for it is emotion and not reason which governs human beings.

Above and left: It is not the crudity of these Muslim prints which makes them remarkable but the fact that they have been printed at all. For 'graven images' are abhorrent to Muslims, who regard them as blasphemous, since only God has the power and authority to create life. Nevertheless these prints were on open sale in a souk in Fez. The themes of Adam and Eve and the Sacrifice of Isaac are strictly Old Testament, reinforcing the biblical commandment of obedience, and are therefore good Muslim ethic. So, though the prints break the edict against graven images, they are not infidel. They are crudely drawn in a style suggesting that the artist had little or no experience in drawing humans, especially nudes.

Block-printed paper. 12×9 ins. Modern. Fez, Morocco. Dan Jones collection.

13

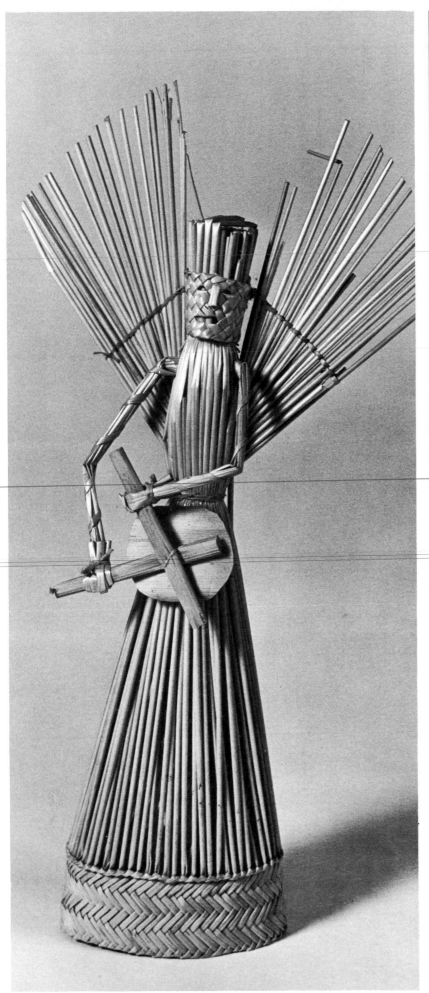

Above and left: In Catholic countries, where 'graven images' abound, peasants readily create spirit symbols from any material available. These Mexican angels are made of straw and palm leaf, twisted and plaited in various textures and thicknesses. Child angels are very common in Mexico, where child mortality is high. The little-girl angel (*above*) has a status-enhancing border on her heavenly garment.
Straw and palm leaf. Height: 15 ins. (left); 8 ins. (above). Modern. Mexico. Author's collection.

Right: Protestants are expected to exercise restraint in the expression of grief for their dead. Yet English churchyards display many grandiose tombstones, the cost of which is often disproportionate to the means of the bereaved family. A 'good send-off', a 'ham funeral', 'we did pa proud' may include a huge marble angel pointing the way to heaven. This not only placates the spirit of the departed but also provides a satisfactory display of status in the community he has left behind.
White marble. 12 ft. 20th century. City of London Cemetery, Forest Hill, London.

Sacred
To The Memory
— OF —
A BELOVED HUSBAND
AND FATHER
George Henry
Charles Reeves
WHO DEPARTED
THIS LIFE
28TH OCTOBER 1936.
AGED 53 YEARS.

TILL WE MEET AGAIN

I CANNOT SAY, AND I WILL NOT SAY,
THAT HE IS DEAD, HE IS JUST AWAY
WITH A CHEERY SMILE AND A WAVE OF THE HAND,
HE HAS WANDERED INTO AN UNKNOWN LAND.

Above: Taoist good luck charm which claims to cure all diseases, prepared by a Taoist priest who wrote the magic formula in lucky red ink on auspicious yellow paper, to be burned and drunk. The joined circles symbolize stars. It reads 'with the aid of the Heavenly Trinity, Shan Tseng, Yu Tsing and Tai Tsing, to chase out the demons, and to revive the dying.
Chinese ink on dyed rice-paper. 9×5 ins. Traditional. China.

Right: Roofs, being easily accessible, are vulnerable to entry by flying demons and need strong magic protection. This demon-scarer has glaring eyes to frighten and extra-long arms to seize. It is a magic 'lightning conductor', tied on the roof to intercept demons bringing misfortune by fire, flood, famine and disease.
Carved, painted wood. Height 36 ins. Traditional; 19th-century example. Nicobar Islands. British Museum, London.

Above: Young children, like primitives, go for the essentials—food and security. From a jumble of 'affluent-society' debris Colin unhesitatingly chose and assembled this collage of his mother. Before the social pressures begin, children observe and express themselves with piercing precision. This is a child's view of his typical East London mum: young, sturdy, hair in curlers, unfettered limbs and reassuringly ample breasts.
Made by Colin, aged 5. Eggbox, toilet-paper rolls, cheese-box lid, match-boxes, coloured paper strips, all painted and glued on sugar-paper. 21×16 ins. 1968. Borough of Newham, East London. Author's collection.

16

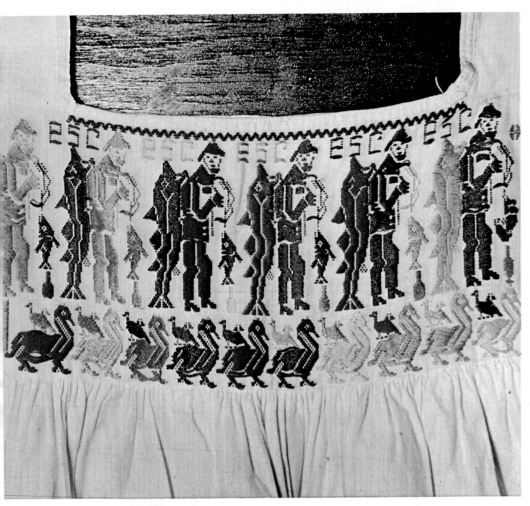

Left: This dance-mask, held by a vertical bar on the inside, combines animist, Buddhist and Hindu symbols. It was worn by the shaman when exorcizing any of the eighteen 'diseases' specified on it (blindness, fever, deafness, stammering, measles, whooping cough, dysentry, cholera, etc.). The patient was purged, sweated and made to fast before the shaman began dancing out the demons causing the disease, to the accompaniment of loud drumming and shrieking. These masks are rare, though still sometimes used in remote Singhalese villages, where the travelling Western medical service is also welcome. Recently, when a mask like this had to be copied for the Colombo Museum, the native carver was too frightened of its power to undertake more than a very little work on it each day, believing himself to be risking infection by contagion with all eighteen diseases.
Carved, painted wood. Height 6 ft. Traditional. Ceylon. British Museum, London.

Above left and above: A truly deep-rooted symbol can be augmented with borrowings from different cultures without endangering its own security, not losing identity but gaining richness. The fish (like the cross, a pagan symbol adopted by the Church of Rome) is a very popular motif in Mexico, where it signifies fertility. The Nahnatl peasant woman who found an empty bottle of Scott's cod-liver oil emulsion was so beguiled by its 'lucky' fish label that she included it in a repeat pattern on the traditional design of her huipil, adding a baby codfish to the fisherman's catch for extra good luck.
Coloured embroidery thread on cotton. Border 16×4 ins. Modern. Huanchinanco district of State of Puebla, Mexico. Courtesy of Miss Irma Johnson. Label by courtesy of Scott and Bowne Limited.

Fertility symbols (*left to right, top to bottom*): sun (Sioux); sun, star and crescent moon (Tunisian tattoo); sun and moon, means 'shining bright' (Sioux); cardinal points, crescent moon and stars (Tunisian tattoo); three cardinal point symbols and sun with rays (stone-age cave drawings, Lovo, Congo); cardinal points, called the 'oil well' (Tunisian tattoo); turning swastika symbol and sun enclosing cardinal points (stone-age cave drawings, Lovo, Congo); sun enclosing turning swastika (American Plains Indian).

Symbols of fertility

The spiral

One of the earliest and most persistent of rain symbols is the spiral. It represents the whirlwind, which brings rain, and is a symbol of prosperity and fertility since rain brings increase. Wherever the spiral form was found in nature it was worshipped as life-giving and beneficent. The whorled shell was held sacred as far back as Palaeolithic times. A devout Hindu mother gives birth with a sacred conch beside her and with a scarlet spiral painted on the door of her room to encourage her, by sympathetic magic, to accomplish the life-producing movements of labour. In Mediterranean lands the spiral form was associated with the octopus and the serpent, which, writhing like the whirlwind and the waterspout, promised life-giving rain. Writhing spiral forms in plants and trees were held sacred for the same reason. The fig-tree, with its writhing trunk, has for thousands of years symbolized fertility. The twining vine is the sacred Hebrew symbol of eternal life. The mistletoe, twining round the oak, was sacred to the Druids, who cut the plant of fertility with a golden sickle shaped like a crescent moon (the moon, personified as female, always being associated with rain, the symbol of fertility).

In ancient Hebrew lore the spiral symbolized the special relationship between the people and Jehovah, their god, a living reminder that they must cling to their god if they wished their god to cling to them. This important Hebrew doctrine was repeated in their sacred spiral male side-curls, still worn in Jerusalem by rabbis and seminary students. The traditional Sabbath loaf is baked in a rising spiral shape. The phylacteries, wound spirally round the left arm in the ritual prayers of devout Jews, are a daily reminder of the meaning of the spiral symbol. The pillars of Solomon's original temple were adorned with spiral carvings, and from there the concept found its way to Rome where it can be seen today in the pillars of St Peter's.

The movement of the rain-bringing Chinese dragon is upwards and spiral. Many people believe that the dragon itself also represented a waterspout. The ancient Chinese symbol of life, the *yang-yin*, is a spiral within a circle, representing the male and female principles interlocked creatively. Traditional Chinese family houses had curved paths leading to the entrance because life-threatening demons shun life-giving spirals and can only proceed in straight lines. In Burma and southern China the Buddha is represented with his head covered by small spiral curls, usually blue (sometimes of real turquoise) because rain comes from the sky.

The legend is that the bare-headed Buddha suffered from the rays of the sun during his search for enlightenment, and the snails, pitying his discomfort and grateful for his protection of all living creatures, covered his head with their shells to protect it from the heat of the sun. Snails, it is worth noting, are also connected with rain.

Snakes and serpents have always been associated with rain. Wonambi, the giant rainbow serpent, was the water symbol of the Australian aborigines. The Hopi Indians had a rain-dance, which they called a rattlesnake-dance. It was performed by priests, who prayed to the snakes and fed them on special food before the ceremony.

Among the Eskimo tribes and the American Indians of the north west the thunder bird was worshipped as a rain god, responsible for lightning and rainfall. The rain resulted from conflict between the thunder bird and a great rattlesnake; lightning from the thunder bird blinking its eyes; and thunder from the bird clapping its wings.

The white peacock of India and the wild turkey of the Australian and American deserts are regarded as fertility symbols because both of them dance in spiral steps before rain falls.

Puebla peasants from the village of Huehuetlilla in Mexico still perform a famous flying dance to bring rain. Suspended on ropes by their feet from a structure like a roofed maypole, they leap, almost fly, head downwards in wide, spiralling, circular movements.

Polynesians, particularly the Maoris of New Zealand, decorated their gods, war canoes, club houses, jade jewellery and tools with coiled spirals, the basic pattern of all their tattooing. Maoris believed that their facial tattoos were the only means whereby their individual spirits could be identified after death and so sent to their merited hereafter.

Underlying all this is the fact that the spiral form is curved and undulating, and therefore peculiarly feminine. All the earliest deities were fertility mother-goddesses.

The sun symbol

The circle is the symbol of the sun, centre of all life and all energy, symbol of eternity. It is the source of all power, adored and feared in hot countries, revered and welcomed in all cold countries.

The sun embodies the Chinese male *yang* principle, being hot, dry and active. In the days of the Aztecs, one man was chosen each year for the great privilege of being sacrificed as ambassador to the sun. In Mexico the sun is still worshipped today as it has been for

The universal magic rain-symbols are particularly important in drought-ridden Australia, home of the modern artist Leonard French. In his huge stained-glass ceilings and in his paintings he uses basic symbols (square, spiral, fret, fish, circle) in infinite variations. French served his apprenticeship to a sign-writer, where he learned the secrets of enduring materials, the use of gold leaf, and the subtleties of proportion. Using totally modern materials, his colours and textures have the dark richness and enamelled bloom of old ikons, but technically they will endure longer.
'Rainbow Serpent' by Leonard French. Enamel on hessian-covered hardboard. 48×36 ins. Modern. Melbourne, Australia. Mrs V. McAllister's collection. Courtesy of the artist.

thousands of years. Each year in northern countries, especially in the mountains where spring comes late and the winters are cruel, rituals are observed to bring back the sun. In the High Tatras of Catholic Poland, the pagan sun-symbol is carved on tables, benches, cradles, spoons and shepherds' crooks, embroidered on women's clothes and men's trousers, and painted inside and outside their cottages.

The early Hindu temples stand on wheels, which, being circular with radiating spokes, symbolize the sun. To throw oneself under the multi-spoked wheels of the Jagarnath (Juggernaut), the great rolling chariot of Orissa, offered a route to paradise for devout Hindus until the British authorities put a stop to the practice.

George Percy, on one of John Smith's expeditions among the American Indian tribes of Virginia, reported in 1607: 'It is a generall rule of these people, when they swere by their God which is the sunne, no Christian will keep their oath better upon this promise. These people have a great reverence for the sunne above all other thing; at the rising and the setting of the same, they sitte downe lifting up their hands and eyes to the sunne, making a round circle on the ground with dried tobacco.'

The moon symbol

The moon has always been connected with magic. It waxes and wanes mysteriously. Its cycle is allied to the tides of ocean and the monthly menstrual cycle of women. In the astral pantheon it is traditionally given a female personality.

Just as the Chinese *yang* sun principle is male, hot, dry and active, so is the Chinese *yin* moon principle female, cool, moist and passive. The *yin* principle has shaped Chinese imperial ritual, ceremonial dress, architecture, canons of beauty and cuisine. Chinese houses have traditional auspicious 'moon' interior doorways. The traditional Chinese hump-backed bridge is, of course, semicircular: reflecting itself in the water below, the moon circle is completed. Not only did Chinese court beauties cultivate crescent 'moon' eyebrows, but the imperial concubines were particularly chosen for their auspicious 'moon' faces, that is they were characteristically flat and circular. Yao Niang, the beautiful imperial concubine who according to tradition introduced the practice of foot-binding, wanted to shape her small feet into crescent 'new moons'. The ritual robes of the Chinese emperors were cut very wide in the sleeves so that when the Emperor raised his arms the sleeve-openings formed perfect circular

Above: Drawn by himself, the moko face of Chief Te Pehi Kupe. Note the life-oriented spirals and cardinal points. Here symbols are being used as identity-definers and 'signatures' (as in heraldry). Maori moko (tattooing) recorded family names, war wounds, etc. It gave status on earth and after death enabled the spirits to identify the dead and send them to their merited paradise.
By Chief Te Pehi Kupe. Ink drawing. 1826. London.

Right: In West Africa the symbol of eternity is a snake biting its own tail. The circle that is created stands for the two united halves of the world. Here it appears on the personal identity door of a Nigerian ruler. When a Nigerian monarch fell from power his personal door was discarded and a new one carved for the incoming ruler.
Carved wood. Section from panel: height 9 ft 2 ins. 19th century. Yoruba tribe, Nigeria.

moon shapes. Even today the Moon Festival is celebrated in China by the eating of specially prepared crescent-shaped 'moon cakes'.

In India a Hindu festival of great antiquity was the 'pole-planting' fertility rite, which took place at the time of the first new moon preceding the vernal equinox, when the pole was crowned and worshipped.

One of the most important Jewish religious symbols is the seven-branched candlestick. Like the Chinese moon-bridge in reverse, this semicircular candlestick forms the lower half of a moon shape, the upper half-circle being devoutly completed in the beholder's imagination to form the perfect full moon.

The rod, the cross and the swastika

The rod, stick, staff and sceptre are symbols of phallic power. The *lingam*, ancient symbol of the transmission of life, was worshipped in India long before the Aryan invasion. The origin of the *lingam* is the digging-stick or primitive plough, since both the plough and the phallus in their different ways prepare for insemination.

The Hindu kings ruled with the Danda or rod of punishment, described as the 'father of morality' and the 'refuge of kings'. It was personified and worshipped as a eunuch deity of power, black-faced, four-fanged, with four arms, eight legs and eyes all round its head.

Krishna, the popular Hindu god of love, plays his flute to the enamoured milkmaids. This symbolizes phallic male power, female receptivity, and the milk of fecundity.

A sovereign cannot reign without his sceptre of power. The House of Commons cannot sit without its mace. The conductor of an orchestra cannot begin the overture without his baton, nor a field marshal take command without his staff of office. Rods are not for women, and when assumed by them are associated with sorcery. Thus witches in Great Britain traditionally fly to their sinister sabbats on broomsticks. In the ballet 'Giselle' the Queen of the Wilis wields two wands; the right-hand one gives her power over her wilis, the distraught ghosts of virgins who died of betrayed love, and the left-hand wand gives her power over mortal men. She uses the power of her left-hand wand by night to make men dance themselves to death, and nothing can arrest her except the holy cross. The symbolism is obvious. But perhaps the power of the cross over the wand may be made clearer.

For the cross is more than the formal cross of Christianity. It symbolizes phallic power in its creative aspect. James Laver, the social historian, holds that the cross symbolizes the received phallus. The wilis represent sexual non-fulfilment. The cross symbolizes sexual fulfilment. That is, the continuity of life triumphs over death.

The cross is much older than Christianity. It symbolizes the yearly renewal of the earth. And the concept of the bleeding young male god dying on the cross to save humanity symbolizes the rain fructifying the earth so that the hidden seeds will grow again in the spring that people may have bread.

The cross is in fact one of the oldest of all symbols. It is the earliest star-map, fixing the four cardinal points. This was a tremendous leap forward in the understanding of stone age man, who followed the seasons in his search for edible plants and game. The North, the South, the East and the West, through this symbol all were laid open to receive the vital winds bringing their rains in their rightful season. In early religions, the cardinal points are male and female, and the Navajo Indians classify rains as he-rains and she-rains.

Movement

The swastika, or the armed cross, symbolizes the movement of the seasons. Turning clockwise, the swastika is life-orientated, fertility-granting, auspicious and lucky 'white' magic-making. The action of sowing seed is from left to right. Turning anti-clockwise, the swastika is life-destroying, demonic, inauspicious and unlucky. The left-handed swastika is used in certain black magic Tantric cults concerned with devil-worship, in the adoration of the goddess Kali in her destructive aspect and for the summoning of male and female demons. The clockwise swastika that Hitler used for the flag of the Nazi Third Reich was advised by his occultists.

The Hebrews believe that God breathed over the still waters and started life into being. The Hindus believe that Shiva, Lord of Creation, danced, and life was stirred into being. And Shiva must continue to dance to keep the universe in ordered movement. Life was created by movement and can only be maintained in movement. Magic power is created by the movement of dancing, like the generation of electricity, and this magic power keeps the world and the heavens in operation. The circular movement is the necessary magic-generating movement. Therefore dervishes whirl. Therefore Europeans waltz. Therefore belly-dancers rotate their stomach-muscles clockwise. Therefore little boys spin round tops. Therefore port always circulates to the left. Therefore Catalonians, in every village

Vegetable-shaped wax candle, moulded in rain-inducing spirals. Carried in Catholic fiesta processions, it is essentially pagan in origin. Pre-Christian rain gods are being invoked, shown what is required of them and for what purpose in this end-product symbol. Today in Mexico traditional wax candles like this are sold in stores and street markets side by side with imported meaningless trash. Fortunately so far the bad has not driven out the good because Mexican peasants are proud of their heritage and sure of their skill. Their handicrafts, as well as being used and appreciated at home, are exports of national importance. *Amber dyed wax. Height 9 ins. Traditional design. Acapulco, Mexico. Author's collection.*

square, dance their ancient *sardanyas*, the circular sun-dance which, with its alternating slow and quick steps, keeps the sun actively shooting out its powerful rays. Therefore Navajo Indians perform their ritual circular sun-dance to keep the sun from slipping. Even the joined hands, so typical of round dances, keep the power contained within the circle.

When the sun entered Aries, sun worshippers in western India hoped to attain early paradise by impaling their bodies on great hooks attached to ropes which were swung in wide circles in the *dola-yātrā* ceremony. The ropes swung clockwise in honour of the circuit of the sun. In ancient times in the *yupa* ceremony, a Vedic priest squatted on a circular disc or wheel placed on the top of the *yupa* (sacrificial post) and was turned in clockwise circles.

Movement, as a generating power, contains magic. Touching or rubbing the right objects is believed to bring the desired luck. The laying on of hands is widely believed to confer magic benefit. Australian aborigines attribute important magic power to touching and rubbing. They had a particularly valued magic pearl-shell disc which came from the northern Queensland coastal waters. These pearl discs were traded for thousands of miles throughout Australia, always for use in fertility ceremonies, when they were rubbed edgewise against the earth. Over the years they would become smaller and thinner until they were only the size of a sixpence but they still retained their immense magic power.

The traditional English maypole dance, which the Puritans forbade as pagan, is a sun-dance to promote fertility. The reason the English Puritans tried to stop village dancing was not that they feared its carnal stimulation, but that they feared its power to generate magic. A pagan force outside their religious jurisdiction was being invoked, and they were afraid of it. No people had a greater awareness of the Devil and his evil powers than the Puritans, who were terrified of witchcraft. Whether the villagers danced clockwise or counter-clockwise, they feared the government was being magically undermined.

Right: The repeating pattern on these popular mass-produced tiles is based on ancient symbols, the rayed-sun enclosed in a cardinal-point square with four planets.
By Peggy Angus. Black on white glazed clay; linocut design. 6×6 ins. Modern. London. Author's collection.

Left: In this 19th-century corn dolly the cross has its original pagan significance, as a fertility symbol. Assembled from the grain of one harvest, kept until replaced by ripe grain from the next harvest, the corn dolly served to remind people that human fertility depends on the fertility of vegetation. There is a current revival of interest in corn dollies, now being developed into a minor rural craft in a few English villages.
Barley, wheat and oats. Height 18 ins. Traditional design. Birchington, Kent. Courtesy of Horniman Museum, London.

Above: This is the tapa of the headman of Savu Savu. Tapa cloth, made from tree bark, is found throughout the Polynesian islands, each island having its own patterns; it is used for bed-covers and hangings. Here the motifs include stars, flowers, and cardinal points. Important are the heavily reinforced borders (quadrupled bands enclosing two further bands) and the repeat patterns, both making strong protective security-seeking magic. All Pacific islands are subject to hurricane.
Painted tapa. 3×10 ft. Traditional design. Figi Islands. Author's collection.

Above: Anything round and bright symbolizes the sun and the sun must always have a smiling face. This earthenware sun-dish, with its rays spotted like stars, was made by a girl of eight. Children, like primitive peoples, are animists. There is no 'it' in their consciousness. Trees, toffee, lorries, letter-boxes, ships, sausages, all are male or female according to their strength and purpose. For them planets have human personalities and human faces, especially Mother Moon and Father Sun.
Made by Elizabeth. Glazed brown earthenware, pattern in slip. Diameter 6 ins. Modern. Junior school in Hammersmith, West London. Author's collection.

Right: Large hook used by the Iatmul tribe of New Guinea to hang up their fishing nets. The Iatmul support themselves by their fishing and so for them a successful catch is vital. They believe that this carving confers magic fertility on the nets through the female fertility symbol of the moon (here doubling as a fish-head with great eyes which will guide fish into the net) and through the sympathetic magic of the mother-and-child image, that is—just as the woman has multiplied so will the fish.
Carved wood. Height 2 ft. 6 ins. Modern. Middle Sepik, New Guinea. Courtesy of Gallery Primitive, Sydney, Australia.

Left: One of several hob trivets forming part of a small built-in oven in an old cottage in East London. Each trivet has a different sun pattern. The association between sun and fire is obvious. Victorian domestic equipment is remarkable for its close, tight decoration, revealing a terror of space, or, put differently, leaving no room for evil spirits or demons to enter.
Cast iron. Diameter 8 ins. Early 19th century. Stepney, East London. Dan Jones collection.

Below: The sun symbol in a tree-fibre mat from Domenica. The method of stitching was introduced by European nuns but the circle symbol itself is Domenican. The central sun is surrounded by two tiers of lesser suns, separated by a snake-like border suggesting rotating movement.
Tree fibre. Diameter 6 ft. Traditional; still in use. Domenica, Windward Islands. Author's collection.

Below: Pagan sun symbols in a construction of modern materials by the 20th-century artist Feliciano Béjar. These 'Magiscopios' would not look out of place in a cathedral.
Designed and made by Feliciano Béjar. Industrial iron, plate glass, moulded metal units and wire. Height 5 ft. Modern. Michoacan, Mexico. Béjar collection.

Right: The El Alamein fountain. When in play, this startlingly beautiful modern fountain suggests the cosmos. Constructed in units like dandelion puffs, the mechanism is of great simplicity. The flow of water from each tube encounters a slight obstruction which flattens and spreads it in dazzling, whirling circles of different sizes.
Metal tubes and water. Modern. Sydney, Australia.

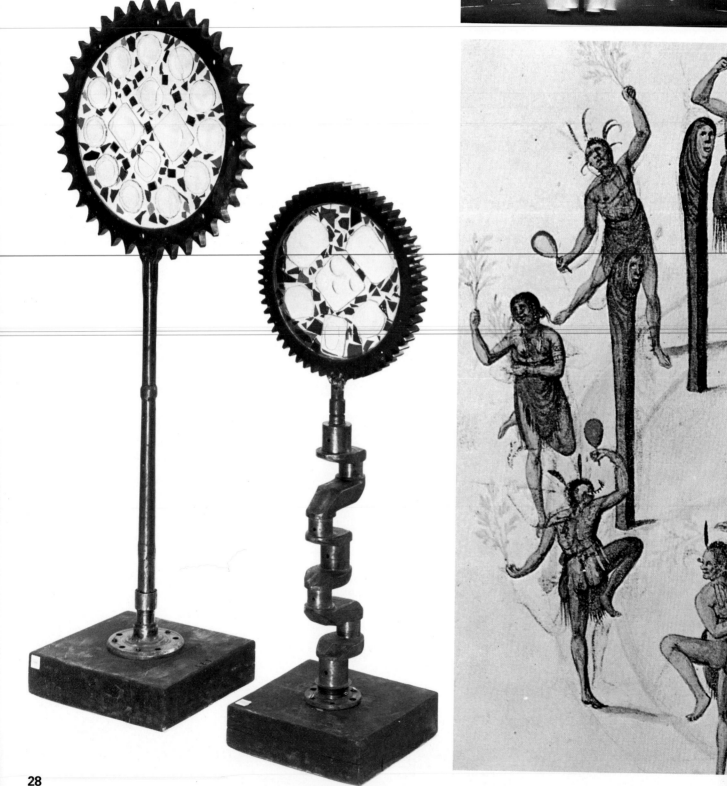

Hindu pilgrims on their way to the Cave of Amarnath, believed
to have once been the home of the Lord Shiva. Pilgrims
undertake arduous, difficult, often costly pilgrimages to
sacred shrines in order to prove their religious zeal and
to gain merit. The more arduous the pilgrimage the greater
the merit. Proximity to a sacred relic, or association
with a holy site, is believed in itself to confer benefit (*darsan*).
The richer pilgrims may travel in litters, on horseback or,
where practical, in wheeled vehicles, but most go on foot.

Gods as symbols

龙 飞 凤 舞
LONG FEI FENG WU

Rain gods

The awesome powers of nature are worshipped in the gods of pagan people. Using whatever materials are available—wood, fibre, seeds, shells (and, after the arrival of the white man, bits of metal, corset-bones, cloth, buttons, mirrors and coins)—primitive people construct extraordinary images of power and terror, closely related to their need for rain and food and children.

In the hot dry countries (India, China, Egypt and the Holy Land, Africa, Mexico and Australia) the need for rain has always been a source of acute anxiety. In these immense areas rain cannot be depended upon to fall when it is required, nor in the necessary quantities, nor in the right places. If the rains fail, crops, herds and humans will starve and die. If the rains fall in excess there will be floods, and crops, herds and humans will be drowned. Therefore in these countries the most potent gods are rain gods, and a multiplicity of images and symbols depict rain, water, clouds, thunder and lightning. The prayers and sacrifices to the rain gods are for regulated rain, rain at the right time, in the right place and in the required quantity.

On the west coast of Africa the most powerful native god is Shango, god of thunder, son of Yemaya, goddess of moisture. Shango has a ram's head (male horns are a fertility symbol) and rides a goat (goats are symbols of sex). The cult of Shango was carried by Nigerian slaves to the West Indies, where today it flourishes, having easily swallowed the official Christian religion. The West Indies, unlike Africa, do not suffer from drought. But they do suffer from hurricanes, another disaster concerning water. The particular task of the West Indian Shango is to control these hurricanes. In all the islands there are little Shango-Baptist churches and holy sites, where altars and fluttering flags proclaim his cult. One such little church in Grenada has four turrets on its roof made from cone-shaped modern fire-extinguishers, painted sky-blue.

The pulling-button of English window shades is traditionally shaped like an acorn. The acorn was the symbol of Thor, god of thunder.

In China the dragon, symbol of the control of wetness, is the most popular and venerated of the deities. The Chinese dragon is compounded of the strengths of several other creatures. It has the head of a camel, the horns of a deer, the eyes of a rabbit, the ears of a water-buffalo, the neck of a snake, the belly of a frog, the claws of an eagle, the scales of a carp and the pads of a tiger. It

dwells amongst clouds, breathing out vital vapours. Ascending, in beneficent spiral writhing movements, it fights with another dragon, and the welcome rain descends from their conflict. Celestial spit from its curling tongue forms the magic sphere which is its attribute, and which is variously named the 'pearl of potentiality', the 'moon', and the 'egg of fertility'. Scholars are still speculating on the origin of this magic sphere, and why it should be so closely associated with the rain-bringing dragon. But the Chinese are an observant and practical people, and perhaps the true explanation of the sphere may be found in Professor Jock Marshall's account of the rain-bringing whirlwind in the deserts of central Australia: 'Often we saw the twisting columns of willie willies (whirlwinds) moving across the land. Sometimes they rolled in their wake a prickly ball of dry vegetation, occasionally a yard in diameter.' The Gobi Desert has similar whirlwinds.

So essential was the dragon symbol to the stability of Imperial China that all the Chinese emperors wore a front-facing five-clawed dragon (that is the dragon in its most powerful aspect) embroidered on all their robes. An ancient Chinese wedding song celebrates the coiffure of the bride: 'On her Head a Coiling Dragon Hair-dress'.

Even today, in the modern China of Mao Tse-tung, the dragon keeps its popularity. The great new bridge which spans a particularly dangerous reach of the unpredictable Yangtse Chiang in Wuhan has a carved stone dragon guarding each end. No festival in China is complete without its dragon-dance, and I have seen, in Communist Peking on the day of the Spring Festival, a municipal tram-car disguised as a dragon, with swaying head, electric eyes, and long jerking tail, chugging along its rails to shouts of joy from the onlookers.

Hong Kong still celebrates its annual dragon-boat race, the original purpose of which was, by sympathetic magic, to remind the rain-inducing dragons to fight each other amongst the clouds, so that the spring planting would be successful.

Since rain is beneficent, associated with fertility and increase, it has become the symbol of good fortune and wealth. In some African rain-dances, the witch-doctor is completely covered with lucky fertility-inducing cowrie shells. The Indian elephant-headed god Ganesh, the most popular of all the many Hindu deities, is the god of fortune, especially renowned for overcoming obstacles. He was originally a Dravidian rain god, white and winged, being associated with rain-bringing winds. In the little booths of wedding photographers in back-street Penang, there are lucky photograph-pictures for sale of Ganesh as bridegroom, in modern evening dress, embracing a beautiful human Hindu bride.

The Aztecs sacrificed human beings to their powerful rain god called Tlaloc, cleaving out their still-beating hearts before his high altar, so that the blood running down the steep steps, like a red river, should remind Tlaloc, of their great need for rain. In Spain images of the crucifixion of Christ are remarkable for their emphasis on the blood pouring from Christ's wounds. Perhaps the strange Christian god Cortés brought with him to the New World did not seem so alien to the Aztecs. Even today Mexican peasants will not protect themselves from the rain, which they regard as lucky.

One of the most revered spirits in the pantheon of the central Australian aborigines was Birrahgnooloo, supreme goddess of water, whose particular sphere of influence was the regulation of floods.

The Hindu ritual pouring of thousands of gallons of milk over a colossal statue of the god Vishnu is a most solemn ceremony. Performed by the highest Brahmin priests, amidst the excited shouting of the populace, its purpose is the same as that of the Aztec ceremony, the African rain-dance and the Chinese dragon-dance. It is an appeal to the appropriate deity to send rain.

In the Temple of Heaven outside Peking, besides the tablets commemorating revered ancestors, there were also tablets for the wind, the rain, for clouds and for thunder, to which the Emperor of China kowtowed and offered sacrifices of food and wine.

Gods must be powerful

People feel safer the more powerful their gods can be seen to be. Asia abounds in colossal Shivas, giant Krishnas and Buddhas the size of mountains; their images are frequently carved out of the rocky sides of mountains or from the inside of mountains. The modern plaster sleeping Buddha in Penang is the length of a street, and the numerous shrines dotted along its length are always crowded with eager worshippers who helped pay its huge cost and are proud to be protected by the largest sleeping Buddha in the world.

Magic power can be expressed by the deity displaying many heads (Ravana the Hindu demon king is credited with one hundred heads) and numerous pairs of arms, each pair of which has the power to perform a different miracle. Sometimes each finger, or position of the finger, of the deity confers a special magic gift. Power is also

expressed by the god being miraculously able to transform himself into any size, shape or substance, and back again, a gift which the Chinese greatly relish in their god Monkey, their version of the Hindu monkey deity Hanuman. Krishna, the god of love, is credited with 16,108 wives and the siring of 180,008 sons. In one adventure he was able to pick up a large mountain with his little finger and hold it like a canopy over his friends for seven days; later in the same adventure he sucked up and extinguished a large forest fire in his mouth.

Buddha, who abhorred images and idolatry, was himself made into an idol upon his death, credited with supernatural powers during his life, and mysteries before his birth. His mother is believed to have carried him for ten months and at birth to have observed he carried thirty-two holy stigmata upon his body. When he left his sleeping wife Yasodhara to pursue his search for truth, it is related that from the far end of the garden he pointed his jade riding-whip at her and she immediately became pregnant. He is credited with the ability to fly and to float up to heaven when he wished to preach to the holy spirits and then float back into life again. And his toothpick sprouted miraculously into a tree. Between his eyebrows he grew white down which had the power of miraculously dissolving hell. In his statues his mystic enlightenment is depicted as a large boss rising from the top of his head.

Protective deities must not only be immensely large and magically potent, but their images must be placed in extremely inaccessible holy shrines, so that, in making painful pilgrimage to these shrines, the worshipper by his sacrifice shows his devotion and will thus acquire merit. In China, Italy, Ireland, India, Ceylon, Africa and Mexico shrines are found at the top of the highest, steepest mountains, sometimes reached by steps cut in the rock, often without even steps or any attempt at hand-rails. The most devoted pilgrims climb fasting, sometimes on their knees.

In China, nothing being considered too good for the idols, and the gods in whose images the idols were carved being able to see everything anyway, it was customary to hide valuable jewels inside them, usually in the head. Buddhist idols often also contained a holy brass mirror and a silk prayer-flag.

Popular clay idols sometimes contained realistic organs—the heart, the lungs and the liver—neatly modelled in silk, veins of differently coloured silk thread and silken bowels carefully wrapped in a piece of satin

Tlaloc, rain god of the Aztecs, 'he who causes germination', double-masked with a triple tier of plumes. This rain deity is usually shown painted black, the colour of priests and magicians. *From a fresco at Tetitla. AD 68–649. Valley of Mexico.*

Left: According to legend, as a baby Krishna stole a butterball from the kitchen one day when his mother was cooking and put it in his mouth. When she opened his mouth to find it the butterball had grown into the universe.
Bronze. Height 2½ ins. Traditional. Madras, India. Author's collection.

Left: Popular image of Shiva. The River Ganges is believed to issue from the toe of the god Vishnu, descending to earth through the potent hair of the god Shiva.
Painted, varnished wood. Height 8½ ins. Traditional design. Bengal, India. Author's collection.

(on the evidence of Dr Dudgeon of the London Mission Hospital in Peking, who in 1879 himself supervized the demolition of certain Chinese idols).

Simple people also want to feel that they can identify with their gods, that someone up there is on their side. The peasants of China associate themselves closely with their magic deity Monkey. They see themselves in Monkey, as they wish to be, and their folk tales are full of Monkey and his adventures: how by diligently studying magic he rises rapidly to become king of all the monkeys, and then by his daring and impudence contrives to steal the sacred peaches of immortality from the celestial gardens and challenges the gods themselves.

Gods bring security

In Africa, despite more than a century of Christian missions and even longer of Muslim infiltration, the native gods are still worshipped. Shango still attracts hordes of devotees to his powerful shrines, including some who live in air-conditioned houses and drive to these shrines in expensive modern motorcars. What they want to know through Shango's priests is what the future will be. As Sigmund Freud has said: 'In fact everything to do with our life is chance, from our origin out of the meeting of spermatozoon and ovum onwards.'

It is precisely this uncertainty, this not knowing what the future holds, which sends human beings scurrying to sacred shrines, temples, synagogues, churches, mosques and fortune-tellers. They want to know if a proposed journey will turn out well or badly; whether a business transaction will be successful or unsuccessful; whether the child they are expecting will be a girl or a boy; whether the battle they are contemplating will be won or lost; whether their sweetheart will be faithful; whether a sick relation will recover or die; whether they will pass their examinations and get the job they want; whether rain will come in time to save their crops; whether they will win the election; whether they will win on the pools; should they press the button?

Security is what people are seeking, and they try to hedge their hopes by closing all avenues of escape for their security. They seek guidance from the most important gods through the services of the most powerful witch-doctors and priests, neglecting no rite and observing all recommended sacrifice. And if the oracle gives them bad news they try to circumvent the approaching ill-luck, by offering up prayers, gifts, mortifications and bribery to sway their gods.

Buddhist temples offer peeps into the future in the form of written spills of fortune picked out, for a small fee, by the temple birds. (Birds are regarded as messengers of the gods.) Fortune-sticks can be cast to answer troublesome questions, and the attendant priest, for a small fee, will interpret the future from the way the sticks fall. Outside the temple in the gardens there are sacred tortoises to be fed in sacred pools, and holy urns where auspicious incense-sticks can be burned. In Bangkok's Wat Pho temple the devout may buy tiny pieces of gold leaf, which they can stick on to whichever feature of the great gold Buddha image they decide will best assist their prayers. Each feature is believed to confer a different boon. The ears, for instance, grant long life.

In Hong Kong what strikes a stranger, amongst the dazzle and glitter, the crochet-covers and bright flowers of the temples, is the number of effigies of anyone who is judged to have achieved fame: great generals, well-known poets, distinguished scholars, important merchants. They are supposed to exude magic power of a beneficial kind, just as do the images of the gods and goddesses. It is a Chinese form of *darsan*, whereby people coming near the source of power will derive benefit from it.

In recent years I have seen in India, on the wall of a desperately poor one-roomed hut in the Western Ghats, the greater half of which was reserved for the emaciated family calf, a coloured picture of a P & O steamer and four playing-cards (king, two queens, and jack). These pictures represented, and therefore exuded, magic power for this Hindu family, who were eager to benefit by being in close contact.

In fact magic is power. Anything which provides power or suggests power can be worshipped. John Smith reported of the Algonquin Indians in Virginia in 1607 that on their first encountering his expedition 'they even worshiped our ordinance, peeces, horses, etc.'

Buddha is everywhere, even in the most remote and least accessible places. Carved into the rock-face so long ago that it has weathered with its matrix, this great standing figure of Buddha is at Bamiyan, on the edge of the Hindu Kush mountain range, which it guards and blesses. The standing position for Buddha is rare and denotes immensely potent magic energy.
Rock. Height 175 ft. 1st century AD. Afghanistan.

To inspire proper confidence in their worshippers, deities must be seen to be very powerful. Multiple arms, multiple legs, multiple heads are used to create symbols of a wide range of magical abilities. Most impressive of all is sheer size. The bigger the idol the more successful he will be in scaring off evil demons. This Wat Chayamangkalaram, claimed to be the largest reclining Buddha in the world, is made of yellow plaster. His features resemble those of a Malaysian business man.
Plaster. Modern. Penang, Malaysia.

Before the invention of man-made materials, natural ones were used to create the great images of deities. Even in decay these images lose nothing of their beauty and impressiveness. This great stone head of Buddha, now overtaken by the jungle over which it once presided, is part of the Tai Som temple near Angkor.
Stone. Tai Som, Cambodia.

Above and far right:
Garuda, half-man half-
eagle, is the mythical
Hindu deity honoured as
the bearer of Vishnu. He
is the son of the Hindu
sage Kasyapa by his wife
Vinyata, who took 500
years to hatch him from a
giant egg. Vinyata hated
her husband's second wife,
Naga Kadru, who had
serpent relations, and in
honour of his mother
Garuda became famous as
a destroyer of serpents.
*(above) Bronze. Height 6
ins. Traditional design.
Ceylon. Author's collection.
(far right) Brass. Height
8 ins. Traditional design.
Tibet. Horniman Museum,
London.*

Right top and bottom:
Engravings illustrating two
of Vishnu's incarnations,
examples of the belief that
a powerful god can assume
different shapes at will. As
Parasurama *(top)*, the
sixth incarnation, he was
taught the use of arms by
Shiva who gave him a
magic battle-axe. With
it he cut off the thousand
arms of the robber king
Kartavirya, who had
stolen the sacred cow of
the sage Jamadagni and
insulted his wife. To
increase his territory
Parasurama drove back the
ocean and cut fissures in
the Ghats with his axe.
Rama *(bottom)* was the
seventh incarnation. He
was the legendary hero
king of the *Ramayana*,
who, aided by Hanuman
the monkey king, slew the
hundred-headed demon
Ravana and regained his
abducted wife Sita.
*Engravings. Mid-19th
century. From Maurice's
'Hindustan', Bombay,
India.*

Left: This popular village
dance-mask from Ceylon,
the fabled Lanka of the
Ramayana where Hanuman
performed his heroic
deeds, salutes both
Hanuman and the sacred
king coconut.
*King coconut. Height
10 ins. Traditional. Ceylon.
Author's collection.*

Right: All Chinese working
people need their own
protective deities, and any
craft which does not
consider itself adequately
covered is entitled to take
over a god and adapt it to
its specific needs. As well
as Buddha the Chinese
have a female Buddha —
Kuan Yin, goddess of
mercy — because the
people felt Buddha too
lofty to cater for those in
need of extraordinary
compassion. Hong Kong
fisherfolk worship a special
version of Kuan Yin,
oriented towards magic
help for fishermen. This
rare and secret image
(*right*) is the very special
version of Kuan Yin
dedicated to the protection
of amahs (housemaids).
She carries a duck in one
hand and a carp in the
other, symbols of felicity
and abundance.
*Gesso and gilding on
carved, painted wood.
Height 5 ins. Traditional;
still in use. Hong Kong.
Josephine Marquand
collection.*

Far right: The traditional
theatre costume of the
popular monkey king in
the Peking opera 'Dis-
turbance in Heaven'. The
monkey deity was intro-
duced into China from
India during the Tang
dynasty. Named Sun Wu
Kung, his astuteness and
audacity make him the idol
of the Chinese common
people. He raised a
monkey army and chatted
his way into heaven where
he stole and ate the
peaches of immortality, so
becoming a god himself.
His celibacy is believed to
bestow magic power on
his wand.

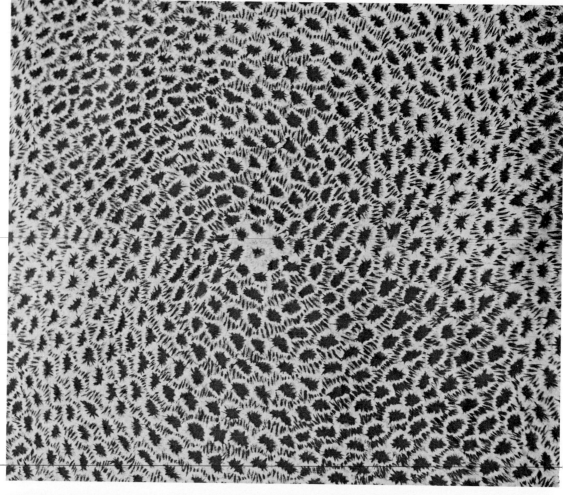

This West African cotton print is based on the ancient African concept of the power of God beneficently radiating outwards from the eternal still centre. Its rich dark colouring, dark brown and dull yellow, suggests an animal skin. The whirling egg-shaped particles suggest fertility and the cosmos.
Printed cotton. 14-in. repeat pattern. 1967. Ivory Coast, West Africa. Author's collection.

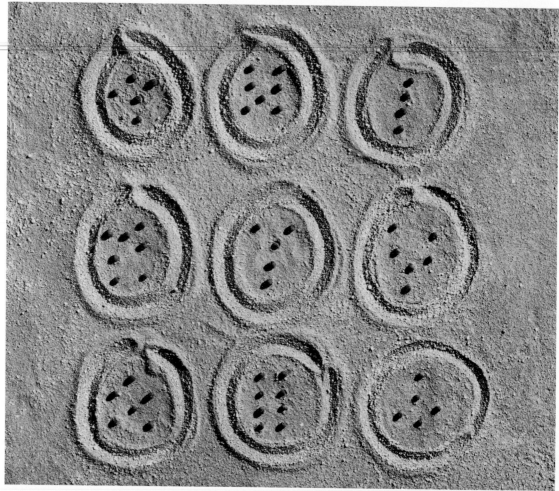

In this African divination ritual practised in Madagascar, the magician drops sacred seeds into circles drawn on the ground, reading the answers to his client's questions by the patterns into which they fall. For greater accuracy this ritual is enacted thrice. The responses shown here read (*left to right, top to bottom*): brother, cattle or goods, asker of the question; spirit of the dead, magician, food; god, father, mother.
Seeds and earth. Variable size. Modern. Madagascar. Musée de l'Homme, Paris.

This porcelain hand is an elegant piece of modern bric-a-brac, telling fortunes according to the wearing of rings on the different fingers. The explanation reads: 'He who wears a ring on his third finger is bound for life. He who slips his ring on to his middle finger is soon to be married. He who usually wears it on his index finger leaves his loved one at the door. He who puts it on his little finger is certain of pleasing.' *Porcelain. Height 9 ins. Modern. Paris. Mitzi Cunliffe collection.*

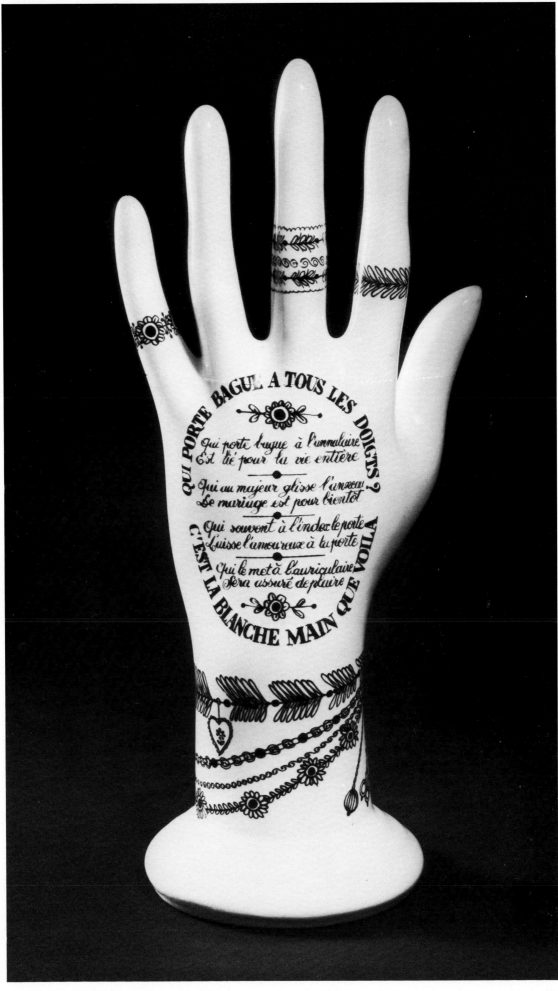

Left: Immense power wrapped in a tiny container is a popular symbol of the awesome forces of nature. This model was recently made at sea by an English officer in the mercantile marine. Though ships are now powered by diesel oil and guided by radar, the sea remains dangerous, and some sailors still practise propitiatory hobbies such as this. *Balsa wood, paper, sewing-cotton, 40-watt electric bulb. Height of ship 1¾ ins. 1968. Author's collection.*

Below and bottom left: The pearl buttons of London's charity-collecting coster kings and queens spell out their territory. Elected by popular choice in the Middle Ages to protect other costers from hooliganism, the rank of London's coster royals became hereditary. The pearl-buttoned insignia date from the late 19th century. Each coster royal must design and sew on his own pearly patterns: stars, bells, flowers, trees of life, teapots, donkey carts, flying birds. lozenges, spirals, 'Faith

Hope & Charity' and the renowned 'Three Pots a Shilling' (a coster love-song immortalized by the music-hall singer Kate Carney).

Above: This *waninga*, made in the Australian desert from vegetable debris, human blood and hair, is the power-conferring insignia of the Ara, or Red Kangaroo tribe. Aborigines belonging to this totem would have special affinities with the Red Kangaroo and with each other. *Wood, feathers, fibre, hair, blood. Height 30 ins. Traditional. Central Australian desert. Adelaide Museum, Australia.*

Above: Signatures of rulers have built-in *darsan*, their upward slant and heavy underscoring revealing the tendency towards megalomania inherent in all holders of high rank.

Popular art in all countries publicises deities, royalties, heroes and high-ranking officials. People like to have images of their rulers. In war-time the features of commanders and allies suddenly become important, and popular plates like this one (*left*) from the 1914–18 War are hurriedly printed, rushed out and eagerly bought up. In British colonies, past and present, effigies of British sovereigns can still be found, stamped on mugs, embroidered on cushions, printed on lengths of dress cotton and carved in heroic marble. A Yoruba carpenter carved this image of the great white Empress Victoria as a fertility goddess. In deference to her wealth and status he took care to give her boots, though they are not seen unless the carving is handled.

(top) Ceramic. Diameter 10 ins. 1914–18. England. Professor Cunliffe's collection.

(bottom) Carved wood. Height 7½ ins. 1880. Nigeria. Author's collection.

Though dominated by the Church of Rome for 400 years, Mexican peasant art is deeply rooted in its rich pagan past. These images of power are painted with symbols of fertility: spirals, clouds and serpents. The king figure holds a small basket in his right hand. The queen clasps an *ixcuintle* (the hairless dog used as a hot-water bottle in illness and also eaten). Her crown is surmounted by a flying bird (the Holy Ghost?) and her painted cheeks are a snide comment on the customs of white women. *Painted, unglazed clay. Height 33 ins. Modern. Tierra Colorada, State of Guerrero, West Mexico. Author's collection.*

In India jewellery comes before dress as a source of magic
protection. Even the poorest Indian woman wears some jewellery. This Lombardi Indian gypsy woman with her child is wearing a forehead amulet, a nose-ring, heavy ear-ornaments,
several necklaces and breast amulets, and many bracelets
and anklets, besides finger-rings. The child is wearing a
breast amulet, ear-ornaments, bracelets, anklets and a magic
protective genital ornament.

Magic protection of body and dwelling

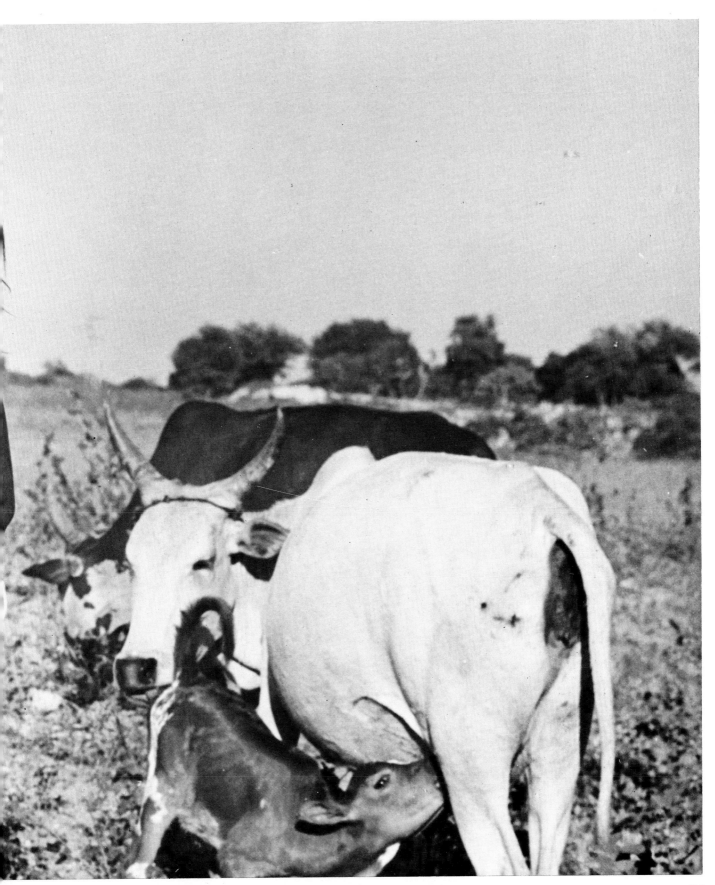

The body

The parts of the human body which require magic protection are the orifices. Like any other openings, human orifices invite entry by demons or evil spirits.

In Arab countries the eyes, especially in young children, are encrusted with magic-protective *kohl* on upper and lower lids. Most primitives protect the nostrils with bone, stone or metal ornaments, and Hindu ladies of wealth wear jewelled nose-rings on both nostrils, and sometimes a third between the other two. Ear entrances are universally protected by ear-rings fastened to the lobes of the ears and sometimes an ear-jewel spiralling round the ear itself. The mouth is often safeguarded by tattooing on either side and also on the chin. Muslim women wear a gauze scarf which is meant to cover the mouth. Lipsticks may also be lucky and protective.

The sexual orifices of the body are regarded as specially vulnerable. They are protected by various devices, such as written or woven charms, sacred life-attaching threads, demon-repellent leaves, penis-wrappers of painted palm-leaf fibre, and jewelled girdles. The real place for the belt is not round the waist but round the loins. The poorest naked Hindu baby boy wears a lucky silver charm-girdle round his genitals.

The *braguette* or codpiece worn, in one form or another, throughout Europe by all classes of men in the fifteenth and sixteenth centuries was for magic protection as much as for gallant assertion. The woollen trousers of Carpathian highland shepherds are richly and boldly embroidered round the crutch.

Apart from the danger of demons and evil spirits creeping into human bodies through their natural orifices, it is also necessary to guard the openings of clothes. The ends of sleeves and trousers, the hems of dresses and shirts, the neck-fastenings, the tops of knee-hose and the sides of stockings, all offer chances of entry to determined demons, and therefore all must be magically reinforced. Embroidered borders guard every edge. Just as nature abhors a vacuum, so do people fear an open space in their garments, as an invitation to bad spirits to leap in.

Ordinary people also like to wear reminders of the gods' power about their persons, such as amulets, which are portable heart-protecting shrines. They feel safer wearing lucky bracelets, lucky anklets, and lucky mirror- and bell-decorated garments, all of which enable their gods to chase away fiends. And to incorporate power-giving movement into their dress, such as

rain-inducing fringes and trembling hair-ornaments, gives them a greater sense of security.

The home

Besides the magic protection of the openings of his body, man has equal need for the magic protection of the openings of his dwelling. Indeed Australian aborigines are so afraid of evil spirits lurking inside any room which has a ceiling that they insist on sleeping outside the house altogether, in the open, where they can light a spirit fire on either side of them to frighten off the demons.

The Chinese believed that demons and evil spirits could only fly in straight lines. This set the style of all religious and most domestic Chinese architecture. The roofs of all important buildings were curved at the corners, to be unnegotiable by flying demons. In addition the roof-beams were crowded with lines of small ceramic protective animals, so that the demons could gain no foothold.

Roofs of holy places, other than Chinese, also have their protective symbols. The steeples of Christian churches are believed to symbolize devout hands joined in prayer, though the original inspiration may have been phallic, signifying life everlasting. The most interesting motifs in Muslim sacred architecture are the cupolas and minarets of their mosques, suggesting the full breasts and virile phalli desired by a warrior religion.

The windows of holy places, such as churches, need strong protection because they are larger and more important than ordinary domestic windows. The stained-glass images of holy saints, which throw coloured reflections amongst the congregation, are a popular method of magic protection. The early Hebrew synagogues were always designed with their casements narrower on the inside than the outside, in order to project and funnel holy power outside the sacred building so that demons might be discouraged from even approaching. In the 1000-year-old Buddhist temple of Mykosan in Korea, there was a great bell, a huge wooden gong and an enormous hollow wooden fish, all three of which were beaten at 3 a.m. at the start of each day's holy services to frighten away demons.

The path to the front door and the door itself needed guarding. The Chinese laid winding paths to keep the demons away. They also, for further protection, set up a 'spirit-wall' in front of the entrance to the house, to introduce unnegotiable corners to defeat the demons. Windows and doors in Chinese house-planning were not placed directly opposite, lest the good spirits, having been coaxed in, flew out again. Windows had also to be heavily shuttered to keep out the night dew, which was believed to have demonic properties.

In China the entrance door, painted a demon-defying red, must be protected from devils with guardian lions and paper door-gods. The Scots grow a red-berried rowan tree outside the door to defy witches.

The most popular doorknockers in England are still lionheaded. They are magic-protective because of the lion's association with power, authority and importance.

Even in England belief in horseshoe magic persists. The horseshoe is nailed on to the door, and it must be nailed open end upwards – not so that the luck may not fall out, but so that the devil may be caught in the curve. And iron has always been regarded as a strongly magic material.

Fireplaces and chimneys are important openings which need careful guarding. In cold climates the fire is the soul of the house. In hot countries the fire of burning incense or the fires of domestic cooking need equally careful protection. In countries where the hearth is open, protective devices appear on both sides and above the fire, and the chimney is heavily guarded against evil spirits. In rural Britain it is traditional for the shelf above the fire to be crowded with protective objects such as a clock (sun-propitious) and family photographs (ancestor-invoking). It is also traditional to hang the door-keys and the almanac near the fireplace, as further safeguards.

But some peoples will not have chimneys, because they believe smoke from fires has magically protective powers. Travellers in Tibet reported that the peasants refused to have chimneys because they regarded the smoke as beneficent and did not wish it to escape. Australian desert aborigines also take a kindly view of smoke, stoking up their fires with green wood to make them smoke more profusely when they wish to smoke themselves and their friends for good luck. Smoke itself has varied values. There is he-smoke and she-smoke. American Indians used smoke to seal treaties, and three puffs of smoke to signalize danger and ask for help.

Some African tribes shape their stools and pillows to protect the spirits of their owners, whether asleep or away. The Chinese emperors used the finest porcelain pillows, shaped like lions, to protect them in sleep, and Chinese peasants observe the same magic practice, with rough ceramic pillow-cats. In rural areas of China counterpanes are made of auspiciously-patterned blue and

white batik, and bed-curtains are embroidered with lucky symbols on lucky red cotton. Animal legs and feet on furniture are a world-wide magic-protective device.

Many people in the East believe that mirrors frighten away devils—because devils fear their magic lightning-flash—so they are widely used. Failing mirrors, in China it is a precaution to place a goldfish bowl opposite the door, where the glitter of the glass combines with the lucky fish-symbol to stop the entrance of demons.

Demon-repellent mirrors are used as mosaic in the pillars and ceilings of the Shwe Dagon pagoda in Rangoon, Burma. Within the famous Rajput Amver palace near Jaipur in India there is one domed room entirely set with small mirrors which has no windows at all, so that it can only be seen by artificial light, usually a candle.

Above and right: Jewellery is a magic-protective device, being designed to protect that part of the body upon which it is fastened. Animals and idols are similarly protected. Necklaces are particularly important because they are mother (encircling) symbols and because they guard the vital head. The necklace of small inset mirrors (*above*) has a lucky fringe of triple pearls and an adjustable cord ending in a lucky red silk tassel. The pendant (*right*) has a lucky fringe of turquoise and pearl.
Mirror, gilt metal, pearls (pendant with turquoise). Diameter of pendant 2 ins. Modern. Jaipur, India. Author's collection.

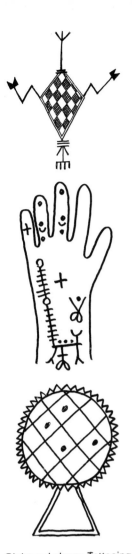

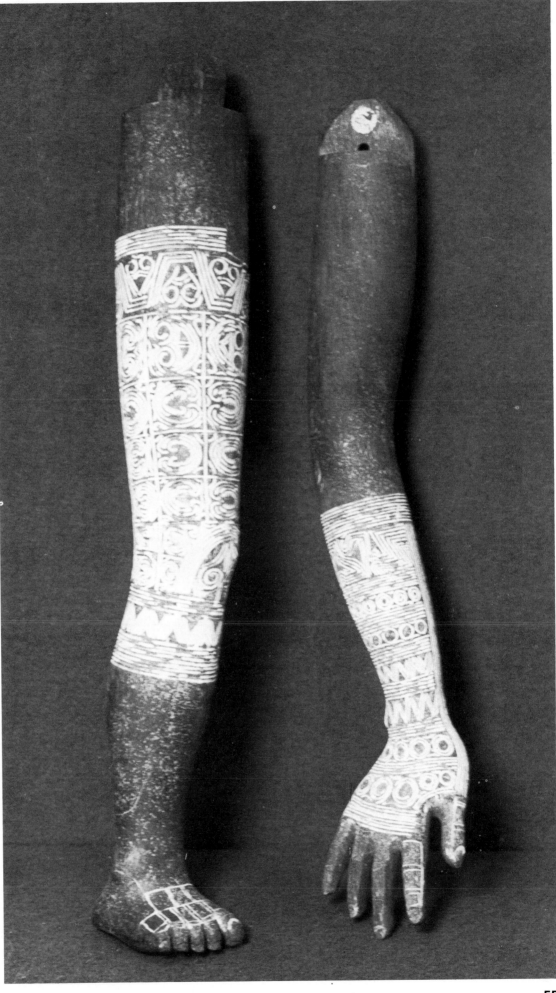

Right and above: Tattooing is universally practised for purposes of self-glorification, identity-establishing, and magic protection from demons, disease and accident. Sailors and soldiers regard tattooing as a certificate of prowess and allegiance. So do thieves. The plaster limbs (*right*) are a Malaya tattoo chart, and the line drawings (*above*) show Tunisian tattoo patterns. Note the eagle, an obvious power symbol, and the mirror-shape, both magic-protective designs. The hand tattoo is prophylactic, carefully indicating the special points to be protected from sprain.
(right) Plaster. Height approx. 20 ins. 19th century. Sarawak, Borneo. Horniman Museum, London.
(above) Height: 6 ins. eagle; 2 ins. mirror. All modern. Tunisia.

The Chinese symbols in these Miaou tribal magic-
protective sleeve borders (coins, serpents, flcwers,
spirals, phoenixes) are exaggerated and hectically
coloured to Miaou taste. Miaou women (from Yunnan,
South China) are famous for embroidery and witchcraft.
Note the security-seeking edgings in the upper design
and the hostile-toothed spikes in the lower one.
Coloured silk embroidery on cotton. Size variable.
Traditional. Yunnan, South China. Author's collection.

The Inns of Court in London have been devoted to the study and practice of English law for many centuries. Though firmly within the Christian tradition, they contain, inside and outside, many symbols of a pagan nature. This magic-protective gateway in Lincoln's Inn leads to the outer gate into Chancery Lane. It displays a gorgon's head (demon-repelling) with staring eyes to frighten away intruders. The ornamental iron-work is wrought in the form of spirals (life-oriented and auspicious). *Stone and iron-work. Height 14 ft. 17th century, rebuilt 19th century. London.*

T
N . G . C .
1818.

WILDY & SONS
Specialists in LAW BOOKS
ANCIENT & MODERN
BOOK BINDING
IN ALL ITS BRANCHES
Established 1830

This fine papercut cock from Poland has magic-protective powers. In Poland, as in China, the peasants have developed papercuts into a richly individual popular art. They are stuck onto the walls or window-panes of their cottages and changed frequently. The most popular themes are the Tree of Life, and cocks and hens, all life-oriented symbols. The interpretation of the symbol is left to the individual and the placing of the comb on this cock has given it a regal appearance.
Cut paper. Width 6½ ins. Modern. Poland. Author's collection.

A mezuzzah is a talismanic case fixed on the doorpost at the entrance of pious Jewish homes to invoke divine blessings and protection. It is touched reverently with the fore-finger, which is then kissed, by those entering or leaving. Traditionally, it contains a copy of Shemah Israel the prayer which Orthodox Jews repeat thrice daily. This modern example, 'Jerusalem the Golden', shows the Holy Name, the six letters spelling Jerusalem, the Crown of God, the Ten Commandments and symbolic bricks. It is mounted on Israeli olive-wood, symbol of peace and unity.
Gilt and olive wood. 7½ × 1¾ ins. Modern. Jerusalem. Author's collection.

The impressive entrance to Luna Park, Sydney, protected by two towers. The mouth is a powerful symbol, and the sensation of being devoured on entering the amusement park through the giant mouth of a colossal gate-way face adds to the prospect of dissipation. The view of this monstrous, slightly sinister, visage across Sydney Harbour is breath-taking. At night it is illuminated.
Wood and painted plaster. 1930. Sydney, Australia.

60

Hindu kolems, symmetrical designs drawn with rice gruel at the entrance to homes and inside shrine rooms. They are popular altars to attract the beneficent attention of particular deities. There are sixty-four classic kolem motifs of astrological significance. Snakes symbolize sex, the lotus purity, the fish riches, triangles pointing downwards femaleness, triangles pointing upwards maleness, three vertically joined upwards-pointing triangles symbolize man. Crosses symbolize the mystic powers of divinity, a vertical line creation, a horizontal line sustenance, a downward line destruction. Each angle of each part of a kolem represents one degree of the power of the planets and their influence on man. By studying kolems the seeker after truth should understand good and evil and be able to repulse evil. No kolems may be drawn during periods of mourning.
Rice gruel. 3 to 4 ft. wide according to location.
Traditional. Bengal and Madras, India.

Four protective female figures, symbolizing industry and virtue, flank this Victorian monument in Brighton. A clock tower combined with a public lavatory, it was erected to celebrate the Jubilee of Queen Victoria. Her portrait and those of the Prince Consort and the Prince and Princess of Wales adorn the four sides of the tower.
Stone, granite, mosaic.
Height 76 ft. 1888.
Brighton, England.

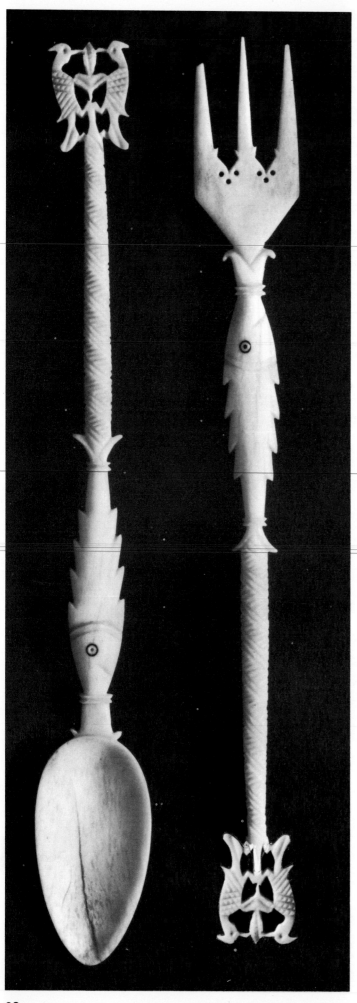

Left: Modern Western people fear infection by germs and viruses. But traditional Eastern people fear infection by evil spirits, and therefore every source of entry into the human body must be magically protected, especially anything to do with food. It is safer to eat with fingers, which must be washed, or personal chopsticks. When other utensils are needed they must be magically protected from demonic influence during the processes of cooking, serving and eating. These ivory servers are heavily reinforced with magic symbols to protect the humans using them, especially at the nearest point of contact with the food. The fish is lucky, and the handles are carved in life-protecting spirals and terminate in growing vegetation guarded by two auspicious birds.
Carved ivory. Length 8 ins. 19th century. Indo-Chinese. Author's collection.

Right: Any object in contact with the mouth needs magic protection against the danger of entry by malignant spirits. This bone toothpick-holder from Nigeria represents a bird or alligator, with rearing watchful head and staring eyes. It is carved with the triangular symbol for male virility (8-fold) and contains holes for eight toothpicks. Eight is considered an auspicious number.
Carved bone. Length 5¾ ins. Modern. Yoruba tribe, Northern Nigeria. Dan Jones collection.

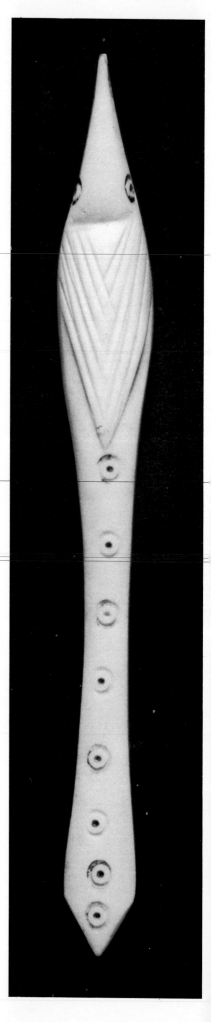

Left: Much of Africa suffers from scarcity of food, tribal taboos on various foods, and widespread terror of poison administered in food by wizards. Mealie porridge or yams are the common diet, both requiring lengthy boiling and hence vigilant surveillance. The bowl and handles of this kitchen spoon and stirrer from Angola are carefully ringed with magic-protective burning to prevent evil spirits entering the food while it is cooking.
Wood. Length: spoon 13½ ins; stirrer 16 ins. Modern. Angola, West Africa. Author's collection.

Above: Not only food comes in contact with the mouth. The accessories of smoking (such as the mouthpieces of hookahs and cigar-holders) can afford entry to lurking demons, by touching the lips, and therefore need magic-protective counter-influence. This elaborate cigar-holder takes the form of three interlaced guardian creatures which form a triple barricade against demons, and the mouthpiece is engraved with a lucky life-oriented spiral.
Silver. Length 5 ins. Modern. North India. Author's collection.

Above and left: Magic-protective borders in the home. This border to a popular Indian cotton-print bed-cover (*above*) shows the Oriental's compulsive use of the device. A border of sword-bearing horsemen is enclosed between two human/ vegetation borders, each bordered by a diamond-repeat border, and topped by an eighth border of flower-filled mango pattern set in a background of leaf-sprays. The double-bordered post Second World War Moldavian rug (*left*) introduces the Picasso peace dove into the centre of the traditional stylized rose-and-lily pattern.

(above) Cotton print. 7×6 ft. Modern. Calcutta, India. Author's collection. (left) Wool. 30×43 ins. Traditional design; made 1952. Kinshinev, Moldavia. Author's collection.

Right: These Polish crochet and embroidery border patterns are based on nuts, plants and common flowers. The decisive translation of natural shapes into highly stylized symbols is a feature of all true peasant art. Strong nationalist emotion, gifted peasants, the shelter of the symbol-oriented Catholic church and the absence of a commercial middle class have enabled Polish popular art triumphantly to survive the pressures of modern mass-production no less than the centuries of tragic wars, invasion and destruction.
Red thread on linen. Variable size. Late 19th century. Silesian Mountains, South Poland. Collected by Elizabeth Taylor.

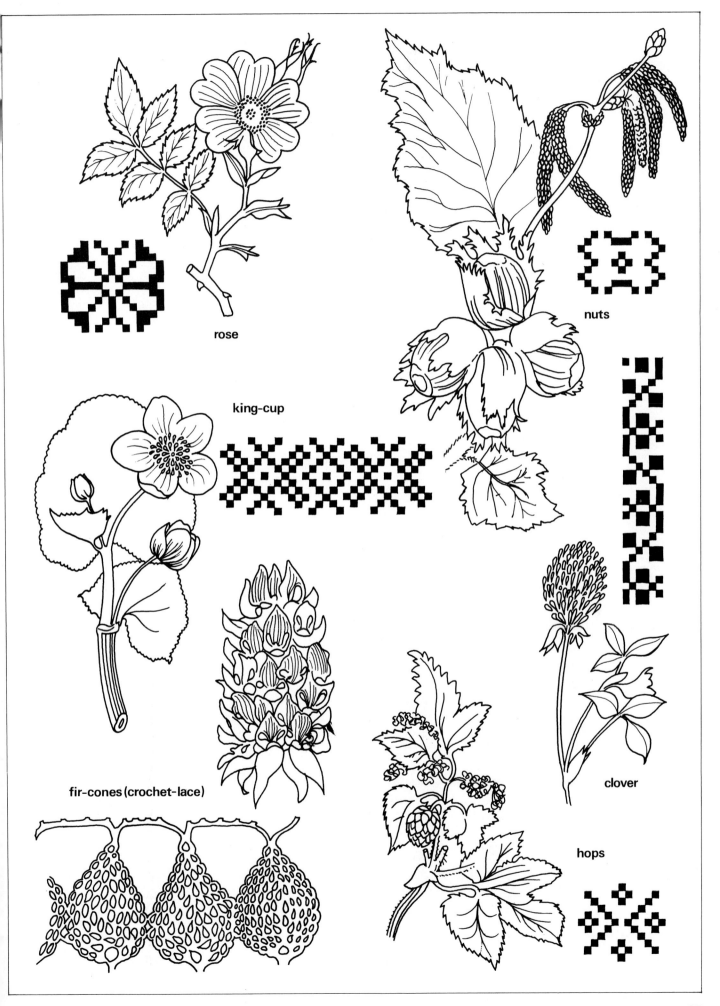

rose

nuts

king-cup

clover

fir-cones (crochet-lace)

hops

Below: Guardian figures are usually made in pairs because the pair induces a sense of safety from threat. Symmetry and repetition are powerful elements in magic-protective symbolism. Paired guardians stand outside doors and gates, are pasted on door-posts, guard the hearth and crouch at each end of the mantelpiece. The horse (one of the seven treasures of Buddhism, element fire, station south) is the Chinese symbol for perseverance and speed. The invading Manchu, in testimony to their victorious cavalry, introduced the pig-tail queue symbolizing the horsetail and the Manchu sleeve based on the shape of the horsehoof.
Bronze. Height 6 ins. Traditional; modern make. Peking, China. Author's collection.

Right: These ceramic spaniels belong to the mining valleys of South Wales, where they are traditionally given to miners as wedding presents. They guard the miner's domestic fire and safeguard his dangerous job. The padlock and chain are security symbols.
White and gold ceramic. Height 9 ins. Traditional. South Wales. Author's collection.

Above: Protective ceramic lions like this pair are popular lucky symbols in China—decorating the entrances to temples, palaces, and the humblest homes. They are made in all sizes and materials. The lioness on the left toys with her cub. The lion on the right plays with a sphere (the sun symbol).
Green and yellow ceramic. Height 5½ ins. Traditional; modern make. Peking, China. Author's collection.

Left: Clay guardian horses from Bengal. To the Indian peasant, horses symbolize power and fertility. White, winged and wise, horses were one of the totemic emblems of early India, though never indigenous. It is believed that Vishnu will appear in his last incarnation as Kalki riding on a white horse.
Polished red clay (sometimes black) with separate ears and tail. All sizes; these 20 ins. Traditional. Bengal, India. Author's collection.

Below: A sun-rayed Mexican mirror showing the use of an active, life-giving symbol for the protection of the home. The sun is the most popular symbol in Mexico. It appears in every church and at every fiesta. The Quetzal dancers of the Puebla highlands and the Guaguas dancers of the Totonac coastal region wear spectacular circular head-dresses, spoked like the rays of the sun and with a circular central mirror in front and behind. They perform a cross-pattern step symbolizing the cardinal points, the rotation of time and the universe.
Tin and mirror. Diameter 16 ins. Traditional. Mexico City. Author's collection.

Right and far right: Protective borders and auspicious fertility patterns on Polish tableware. Note the boldness of the borders and the thrusting vitality of the central motifs. This plate and the one opposite are unique. They were painted spontaneously on biscuit-fired clay by a peasant woman visiting Professor Wanda Telekowska at the Warsaw Institute of Industrial Design which she directs. It is the aim of this institute to encourage and harness the creativity of Polish popular art for the enrichment of modern mass-production.
Blue and white glazed ceramic. Diameter 9½ ins. Modern. Warsaw, Poland. Author's collection.

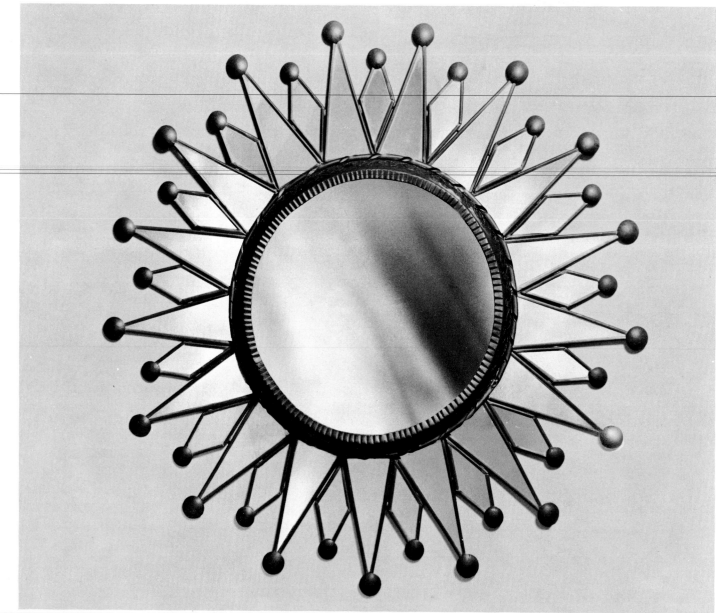

Below: Corners need special protection. This corner detail from a handsome plasterwork ceiling shows the desire for magic protection of the dwelling in early 20th-century Australia. Here European-style foliage ornament of the late 19th century incorporates the Australian protective symbol, the kookaburra—a snake-attacking bird encouraged by householders.
Plaster. 1910. Sitting room of New South Wales house, Australia. Courtesy of Major John de Telega.

Left: The moon-pattern in this popular Chinese rice-bowl expresses a prayer and hope that the rice-bowl may never lack rice. The bowl is decorated by pressing grains of rice into the wet clay; at the first firing the grains fall out leaving holes which become tiny windows when the bowl is glazed inside and outside at the second firing. The border of lucky bats inside the bowl is the traditional Chinese symbol for happiness and longevity.
Ceramic. All sizes. Traditional; still in use. China.

Left: This mother-and-child teapot is specially made for English narrow-boat canal families. Promising success and fertility, it guards and embellishes their homes, a tiny cabin in the rear of the boat.
Glazed brown earthenware. Height 12 ins. Traditional; still in use. England. Mitzi Cunliffe collection.

Below: Nature abhors a vacuum. Peasants dislike empty space, making sure to decorate all domestic surfaces. Painting lucky symbols all over an object keeps at bay the evil spirits. East European peasants, especially the older women, are gifted free-hand decorators. Sun symbols, floral borders, planets, spirals, rain symbols and rooted vegetation decorate this wardrobe painted by a 70-year-old peasant woman from Slovakia. This form of clothes chest is a village bridal present.
Wood, painted brown with designs in white, ochre, green and yellow. 6×5 ft. 1899. Čataj, West Slovakia.

Right: Treasure needs protection against thieves and evil spirits; therefore the shape of jewel-boxes is important. This lacquered owl magically guards its contents against *Nats*, the demons who harry Burma.
Black and gold lacquer. Height 3 ins. Traditional; modern make. Rangoon, Burma. Author's collection.

Left: Emperors and peasants alike need magic protection from demons, especially during sleep. The pillow of the Emperor of China was moulded in the form of a cat by the most eminent potter and painted by the most distinguished artist. The cat-shape was chosen because in China cats are believed to put evil spirits to flight. This common ceramic pillow-cat with watchful staring eyes is a humble version of the splendid porcelain imperial pillow-cat and performs exactly the same police duty.
Brown and white glazed ceramic. Length 8½ ins. Traditional. North China. Author's collection.

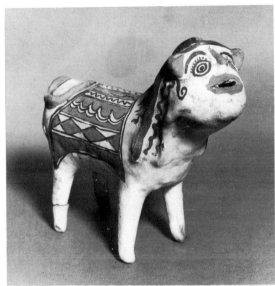

Left: This Victorian glass vase in the classic style, now used as a table lamp, is protectively painted with spirals, acanthus and cardinal points, and bordered with wave and meander patterns.
White glass painted in black. Height 13 ins. 19th century. England. Author's collection.

Above: This magically protected money-box is in the form of a mule with the snarling head of a demoness who guards the contents against thieves and evil spirits. The part which holds the money is painted with water- and fertility-symbol borders.
Painted, unglazed clay. Height 5 ins. Traditional. Tierra Colorada, State of Guerrero, Mexico. Author's collection.

African tribesmen performing their last dance before becoming junior elders. Primitive people try to leave nothing to chance. Every stage of life is carefully prepared for by secret ordeals designed to accustom them to the harsh duties they will have to undertake. Lessons during initiation include the teaching of stoicism in suffering.

rtility and childbirth

The sovereign symbolizes his people and must therefore be fertile, and be seen to be fertile. An Indian king was expected to indulge in water sports in which he was rowed in a yoni-shaped boat with his consort, while he squirted her with water from a golden syringe.

In Malaya fertility of field and family are not separated, and, when the ceremony of sowing is started, it is the local midwife who is called upon to plant the first seedling.

When a child is being born, the midwife must see that all knots and fastenings are untied, sympathetic magic to ensure that there will be no obstruction to the birth. But this leaves dangerous openings through which demons might enter; therefore extra magic protection is sought by prayers and propitiation, and a continual loud noise is kept up, by drumming, wailing, shouting and the explosion of fire-crackers.

Children

Girls being universally less valued than boys, every device was used, both in Asia and in Europe, to trick the demons into believing the boy child was really a girl child. In Europe as recently as a century ago boys were dressed as girls until the age of seven. In Asia the protection from demons was carried still further. The boys would be dressed as though they were girls and hung about with demon-scaring amulets and mirrors; lucky locks would be fastened about their necks to lock them into life; and a belled anklet would be fastened round one foot to frighten away devils. Their survival was supplicated by longevity necklaces of peachwood and peachstones, and sewn into their dress were magic-protective spells, auspiciously printed on lucky red or yellow paper and auspiciously folded into lucky triangles. Their horoscopes, engraved on metal plates, were fastened on to their breasts for further security. The baby carrier of lucky red cotton is still embroidered with auspicious symbols in Hong Kong.

Not only was the baby boy called by a girl's name for years to outwit the demons, but he was given a variety of names, some of which were too secret ever to be used at all. This custom is still practised today in many African communities.

A name is regarded as an actual part of the child, like an arm or an eye, and therefore needs particular magic protection. Reporting the death of Haim Moshe Shapiro, Israel's Minister of the Interior, *The Times* noted: 'The "Haim" now given as one of his names was not given him by his parents. There is an ancient rabbinical custom, the purpose and origin of which are not quite clear, by which the name of a Jew whose life is endangered is changed, or partly changed, with the object of improving his chances of escaping danger. Israel's Chief Rabbis Herzog and Nissim invoked this tradition after it was made known that Moshe Shapiro, one of five Ministers of the Government injured when a mentally unbalanced young man threw a bomb in 1957 from the visitors' gallery of the Knesset to the floor of the Chamber, was in danger of losing his life. The name "haim" in Hebrew means "life".'

In Haiti when a child is seriously ill it is the custom to place it, together with food, in a shallow grave and cover the child with a white sheet, after which a proper funeral service is conducted. This pretend funeral is believed to satisfy the demons that the child has really died, and the patient is then able to recover his health.

Initiation

When a male child is born in the West, the parents, if they can afford it, take out insurance for his education. They have him immunized and inoculated and put his name down for a 'good school'. Twice a year they take him to a dentist. But they do not attempt to arrange his marriage, nor, when he reaches puberty, do they solemnly and with fearful ceremony initiate him into the mysteries of sex and his male rôle in life.

It is not so elsewhere. In Asia the precise moment of his birth is carefully noted so that the astrologer may prepare his horoscope. And throughout his life this horoscope will be closely consulted at every step he takes, most particularly in regard to his marriage, which will have been planned for him at the time of his birth (indeed sometimes even before), for it is vital that his horoscope and that of his intended bride should be magically compatible. Often he will not see her until the wedding ceremony is ver, for she will be heavily veiled.

In primitive tribes (and we must not overlook the ordeal traditionally meted out to new boys at British public schools) the boys have to learn to face starvation, terror and physical ordeals beyond their strength. They must undergo tests and ordeals calculated to force upon them the realities and demands of manhood, all the more onerous since, as boys, they have been petted and singled out for indulgences and relieved of all duties up to this moment.

American Indian tribes, at the end of frightening initiation rites, would send the youth away alone into the woods, where for days he fasted, staring at the sun until his imagination became inflamed so that he dreamed a dream in which he found himself a new name and thus achieved his individuality, with his own device, his own song and his own manhood.

British Columbian tribal initiation rites introduce the youth to his ancestral totem, to the fearful whistling spirit-noises, masked dancing and flaming night fires.

The most interesting of all initiation ceremonies, and the most prolonged, are those of the Australian desert aborigines, whose survival in physical conditions of the most extreme deprivation and austerity is only possible because the initiation rites prepare them for it. There are nine different stages to a boy's initiation, each lasting weeks, and the whole process extends over many years, as he learns and endures enough at each successive stage to permit him to enter the next stage. The actual circumcision is not performed until he has reached the fourth stage. Finally he gains the privilege of wearing the adult's sacred necklace of pearl shells and kangaroo teeth and may then take a wife. By the time he has graduated and is permitted to have sexual relations with a woman, he may be almost middle-aged.

All the initiation rituals start at sun-down. The assembled men and youths gather in large double circles, and the ritual is danced in rotating coils and circuits symbolizing the sun and the whirlwind. Patterns in bird-down fixed to the body with the youth's own blood mark each stage of initiation. The actual circumcision is performed in the midday sunlight, after which the youth is entitled to wear different ornaments, including a chignon of emu feathers and a belt with pubic tassels. After a year of ritual which includes food taboos and blood-drinking (his own and his relations' blood), night vigils, and an ordeal of terror during which ancestral spirits speak to him through the bull-roarer, he must show himself to many remote little groups of relations and walk about 150 miles in the process, no women or children being allowed to go near nor speak to him.

Medals must be earned

Hunting and warfare are primitive pursuits, however glorified by tradition and enhanced by science. Amongst primitives, the hunter and the warrior are entitled to wear or display trophies only if they have seized them in personal combat.

The tribes along the north-eastern frontier of India have strict rules on personal valour which include control of the work of their artists. Only he who has killed a tiger may carve one on the men's club-house, and only

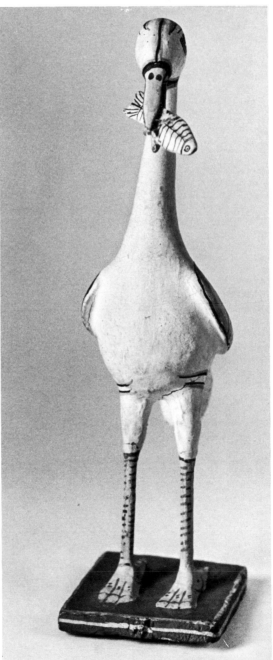

Left and above: These toys, the British butcher's shop and the Indian bird with fish, share an intention: wish-fulfilment through magic, a prayer (to vastly different deities) for food and plenty. They explain to the appropriate gods precisely what they are expected to provide. The traditional Indian toy links animal and human life. The bird has human eyes and eyebrows and curiously human toes. All creatures, both human and animal, need sustenance. The butcher's shop was a toy for well-fed, self-assured Victorian middle-class children whose portion was to be much more than enough. The Victorians, so prudish about the human body, are here brazenly explicit in the luscious detail of the outsize animal carcasses. *(above) Painted, carved wood. 36 × 25 ins. 1840. England. Professor Cunliffe collection. (left) Painted wood. Height 8 ins. Traditional; modern make. Bengal, India. Author's collection.*

Above: If his fishing fails he and his family will starve. The Esquimo harpooner who carved this fine work was showing the gods what he needed, using debris from a successful former hunt.
Weather-pitted fish bone. Height 18 ins. Modern. Esquimo. Gallery Primitive, Sydney, Australia.

Top: No fodder no milk. By sympathetic magic Swedish peasants demonstrate their need: assurance of fodder for their livestock so that they also will have food.
Straw. Height 6 ins. Traditional. Sweden. Horniman Museum, London.

he who has taken a human head in a tribal raid may carve the likeness of a human head.

Chinese generals wore their battle-honours as an array of flags fixed above the shoulders of their uniforms like wings, each flag indicating the number of enemy captured in previous battles.

The Sioux tribes of North America wore trophies of their success in the hunt and in battle. The scalps they had personally taken were hung on a 'scalp-pole', and the scalp-locks they had cut from the heads of their enemies were sewn into the seams of their deerskin garments. Round their necks they were entitled to wear necklaces of grizzly-bear claws, provided they had themselves slain the bear. Their chiefs, who were chosen for their skill and ferocity in war, were entitled to wear the crown of eagle feathers, with pendant feathers reaching from neck to feet. The fierce character of the eagle was believed to confer magic power, and even the chief's horses had eagle feathers attached to mane and tail to confer magic speed and success in attack. Eagles were sacred birds, never killed. The Sioux obtained their eagle feathers from captive eagles.

Ethiopian soldiers displayed their prowess in battle by cutting off the testicles of their victims and attaching them to their lances. They believed that this act was not only proof of their valour, but that it also magically transferred to them their victim's power and at the same time stopped his ghost from taking revenge.

Until 1870 at least, the Japanese soldier wore a foxtail attached to the rear of his uniform, to ensure success in battle and to frighten his enemies.

An interesting aspect of military history was the 'bull's pestle' swagger cane, sported by the officers of the British campaign in North Africa in the Second World War. This was made from the penis of a bull.

There are many forms of 'citation of valour', and the picture-writing of the American Indian lent itself to the depiction of battle successes, in detailed symbols, on the deerskin garments of famous fighters.

Sailors have their own magic symbols of bravery and endurance. At least 50 per cent of sailors are tattooed, in itself a painful process. Traditionally, feathered birds are most popular—the tattoo of a bluebird representing the achievement of 5,000 miles service at sea. The next 5,000 miles is marked with the tattooing of a heart.

Magic food and medicine

All peoples have magic prohibitions about food. Some foods are lucky and some foods are unlucky. Some food may not be eaten because of totemic vetos and some foods are forbidden by religious veto. Even in modern Western civilization the interest in diet goes far beyond the need to slim, and there is always a strong, if furtive, interest in what are believed to be aphrodisiac foods, such as winkles. Even such an innocent custom as pancakes on Shrove Tuesday has deeper magic significance. It is really a spring fertility rite concerning eggs.

The coconut is sacred to the Hindu and also revered by Buddhists. Cupola-shaped marriage archways, made from coco-palm leaves and topped with a plumed coconut, are erected across village roads, as are demon-repellent ceremonial archways. Coconuts are given to all the guests at weddings as a symbol of fertility, especially to women who desire pregnancy, for the coconut symbolizes *bindu* (readiness for impregnation). It also symbolizes the human head, which is sacred, and therefore a coconut may not be broken in the presence of a pregnant woman, lest her child's head be injured. Garlanded and adorned, the coconut is worshipped as sacred to the god Shiva, and on this account it has its own special festival in July/August, just before the monsoons, which is designed to encourage the rains.

Magic medicines, whatever their supposed virtue, are almost always concerned with virility. For thousands of years the Chinese have prepared concoctions made from rhino-horn, deer-horn or ginseng (a Korean root). All are phallic in shape, and therefore, it was thought, they should make good aphrodisiacs. Ginseng is sold today wherever there is a settlement of Chinese. Chemists' shops in sophisticated San Francisco keep it in stock.

No less persistent is the Chinese belief in the magically strengthening powers of tigers. 'Tiger Balm', that universal ointment, is sold all over Asia and Africa. An English resident in Malaya recently watched an important Chinese doctor supervize the reduction of a dead tiger to medicine. Not an item was wasted. The whiskers, claws, and sex organs were first removed for special treatment because their efficacy was strongest. After skinning, the body of the tiger was chopped up, boiled for seven days, and the liquid drained off; then the process of reduction was continued for a further seven days while special prayers were offered for sanctification. The liquid was drained off once more and the residue spread out to dry in the tropical sun. When dry it was pounded into a fine powder, which was sold in packages at five dollars an ounce as the strongest aphrodisiac procurable, having been prepared by a 'real' doctor. So absolute is the

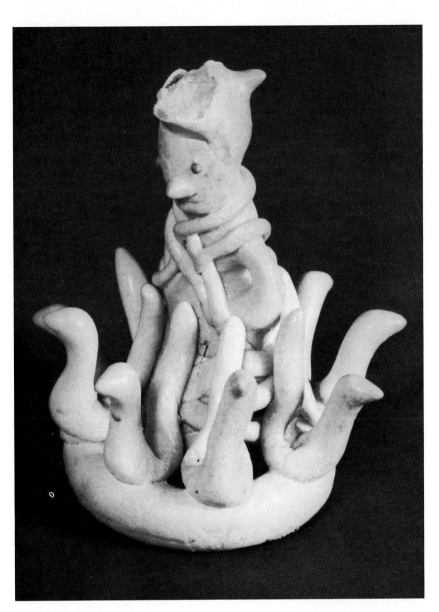

This Polish Easter biscuit is baked in the shape of a farmer's wife with her geese: an appeal to God for good harvests and increasing livestock. There is paganism in this association of the resurrection of Christ with the sprouting of planted seeds. *Baked dough. Height 1–2 ins. Traditional; still made. Poland. Horniman Museum, London.*

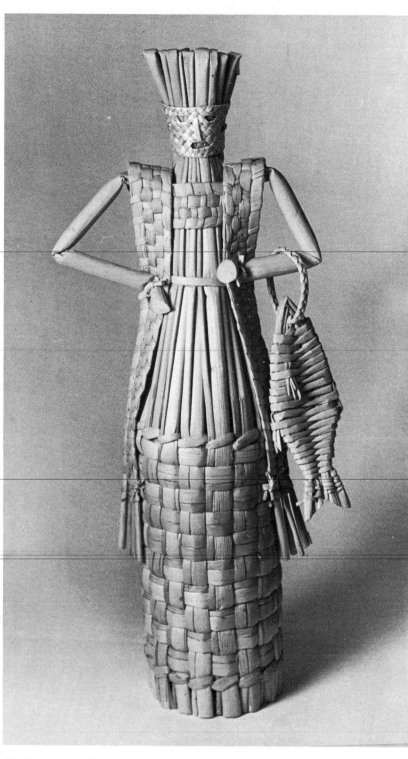

This fisherwoman from
Mexico with her catch is
showing the deity what
she needs.
*Plaited palm leaf. Height
16 ins. Traditional design;
modern make. Coàstal
villages near Acapulco,
Mexico. Author's collection.*

Chinese belief in the magic properties of
tigers that baby boys wear special eared
tiger-caps to give them strength.

Colours

Colours have significance. Red is lucky
throughout Asia because it is thought to be
life-granting. It is the most popular colour
for baby clothes. The traditional Chinese
bridal dress is a crimson satin jacket and
trousers, glittering with demon-repellent
magic symbols, and the bride is carried to her
wedding in a red palanquin.

Yellow is the imperial colour, sacred to the
Emperor. It is the colour of fecundity, re-
lating to the yellow sun and the yellow earth.

In the East where the colour of mourning
is white, white garments do not suggest
virginity and innocence but death and
devilry. White is the colour Australian
aborigines use to indicate the world of
spirits. They draw heavy white lines round
their designs, especially human forms, perhaps indicating that the spirit world begins
immediately outside the human body and is
everywhere. An old Hindu lady in a white
cotton sari is proclaiming her widowhood—
and she may have been wearing this white
mourning dress, without jewels, for most of
her life.

Black, on the other hand, is not associated
with mourning at all in the East, and little
children, even babies, may wear black.

Eyes

In the evolution of man from animal, eyes
seem to have retained their animal-hypnotic
power. Psychotics whose personalities are
disintegrating incessantly draw staring eyes
in asylums for the insane. New-born babies,
as soon as they can see, are transfixed by
human eyes. Even two horizontal spots
drawn on a piece of paper can hypnotize
them. Perhaps this atavistic animal emotion
accounts for the terror of the 'evil eye'.

The power of the evil eye is universally
feared. It is in fact a looked curse. Re-
pellents vary. Muslims put their trust in an
amulet known as the 'hand of Fatimah'. This
holy hand, carefully stylized in order to avoid
the impiety of the graven image, represents
the magic-protective hand of Fatimah, wife
of the prophet Mohammed. For even more
powerful protection a doll-sized ceramic eye
may be stuck onto the hand. This signifies:
'This holy hand repulses your evil eye and
this eye returns your evil curse.'

Spitting, wearing red, carrying salt or a
piece of coal in the pocket were also believed
to counteract the evil eye. Jews once protected their children against the evil eye by
standing them in the smoke of the auspicious

Sabbath candles. Children wear bracelets of double and triple magic eyes to throw back and intensify the looked curse. Adults wear necklaces of multiple eyes, amulets, talismans and tattooed magic designs.

India is the home of the belief in the invisible third eye, situated on the forehead between the eyebrows and just above them. This third eye is a focus of extremely great occult power. Hindu caste marks and the *tilaka* of Hindu married women are sited there. The Angami Nagas of Assam cover it with a small leaf to protect it from the gaze of others. The all-powerful third eye of Shiva is believed to be able to destroy the entire universe in one flash and according to Hindu legend did on one occasion reduce the god Kama to ashes by a single glance.

Tools of trade

Horse brasses, which came to Europe from the Saracens at the time of the Crusades, are traditionally cast in magic-protective designs of astrological symbolism, the sun, the moon and the stars being most popular. Camels wear their own protective amulets, and they are sometimes also tattooed with protective magic symbols for additional security. Mules wear demon-repellent charms, containing a mirror if possible, some fertility symbol and demon-frightening bells. Even the modern motorcar, when driven in the Near East by an Arab chauffeur, will be protected from misfortune by a blue-beaded charm dangling over the windscreen.

The prows of Chinese fishing-junks are traditionally painted with large eyes to enable them to see their way and to locate the shoals of fish. The prows of Chinese war-junks were also painted with goggling demon eyes, to terrify the enemy. The figure-heads of European sailing ships, often female, were intended for supernatural protection from the elements. Even today, Portuguese fishing vessels display life-guarding horns above the pilot's cabin to protect the ship from harm.

Peasants feel less apprehensive when the tools of their trade are decorated with protective symbols. And they like to safeguard with protective patterns the utensils in which food is cooked and the implements with which it is eaten.

In Mexico the important and ancient craft of weaving is saturated with magic. The whole process is regarded as an exercise in fertility-making, the loom being female, the heddle male. Thread is equated with potent female hair and water-bringing sacred serpents. Before weaving is begun, food is offered to the hank of wool to be used, lest its spirit should be offended and bring harm to the household and the village fertility.

Animism

Primitive people are animists. They believe there is life in all things, a life force which will act beneficently or malevolently according to how humans behave. There is no 'it' in their conception, since all things have life and all life has sex. Stones, caves, holes, smoke, tools, wells, trees, winds, all contain spirits which will revenge themselves if neglected or wrongly used.

Trees must not be cut down without prayers and permission from the resident spirit. Animals must not be hunted, nor fish caught, nor wild berries gathered for food, without prayers of propitiation to the spirits of the game and the spirit of the bushes. And, if the hunting, the fishing, the food-gathering are successful, these spirits must be thanked in further prayers, libations and sacrifice. Above all it is essential that the spirits should be assured that only the minimum game has been taken, fish caught, and berries picked, that no morsel of what has been taken will be wasted, and that every scrap, including the skin, will be used, and used economically. Or wronged nature will revenge herself. The spirits will be angry and blight their crops, scatter their game and send their fish far away into waters outside their territorial boundaries, so that they will be punished by starvation.

As we now understand, there is a basis of sound sense in these beliefs. We know to our cost that thoughtless over-cropping of land, forest or water results in erosion, the soil blowing away from the enfeebled treeless earth, and the waters becoming polluted.

Black magic

If white or life-enhancing magic is unavailing, then there is always the chance that black magic may achieve one's ends. And, especially in countries where poverty and insecurity are endemic, some people will always be prepared to imperil their souls in order to prolong their lives and grow rich at the expense of others.

Chinese *Ku*, which flourished among the Miao tribes of Yunnan, is an example of such black, or left-handed, magic. *Ku* witches compounded a poison from three poisonous insects which fought each other in an enclosed vessel, leaving the victor full of all three poisons. This is curiously akin to Chinese planting technique, when three seeds are planted and the strongest of the three plants chosen for replanting. The effect of *Ku* was always to cause fatal intestinal diseases. Yunnan is tropical and marshy; intestinal diseases have long been endemic there, and the *Ku* spirits said to float in the air at night like bright glow-worms could of course easily be the hallucinations of some-one suffering from a disordered liver.

The practice of *Ku* was very profitable. *Ku* witches, apart from taking 30 per cent of the victim's wealth, charged five ounces of silver for poisoning an official's servant and fifty ounces of silver for poisoning an official. If the fee was not forthcoming the witches would turn on their hirer. They were believed to be able to turn themselves into the likeness of pigs which, when eaten by the victim, caused haemorrhage and death, or into foxes with the power of becoming enticing females by night to lure their victims to destruction. They were said to spit fire-balls from their mouths and suck out the souls of their victims so that they themselves could live for a thousand years, always in luxury. People also believed that official statues of horses could be made, under *Ku* influence, to travel by night and attack selected victims, and that funeral stones, old trees, rocks and even porcelain pillows could turn into human form and attack the desired victims.

To safeguard oneself against *Ku* poisoning it was essential to live in an auspicious place: at the end of a street or spiral path, where the demons could not turn the corner, or beside a bridge because they could not endure running water. There were also recommended antidotes: bronze chopsticks (which turned black if there was poison in the food), thunderstones (prehistoric stone axes), the company of striped cats (lucky as they resembled tigers), and hens in the house, for hens were believed to detect the presence of *Ku* poison.

But none of this helped much. *Ku* poison kept its properties and could be used generation after generation. *Ku* witches handed on the poison to their daughters as dowries. It was hard to rid oneself of *Ku* when necessary (during an official investigation for instance), for it could not be destroyed by water, fire or metal. Usually it was given away, left by the roadside in an attractive basket with gold and silver to tempt the passers-by.

In Hong Kong today there are periodic complaints from the poorer Chinese population that their drinking water is infected by 'worms'. Officials inspect the municipal supplies and find them pure. And the *Ku*-inspired terror dies down for a while.

But the practice of black magic is not confined to the poor and oppressed. In modern Britain we are witnessing an increased interest in black magic and reports such as that of a child's corpse being used for rites in a Southwark cemetery (*Evening Standard*, 29 July 1970) are not so uncommon.

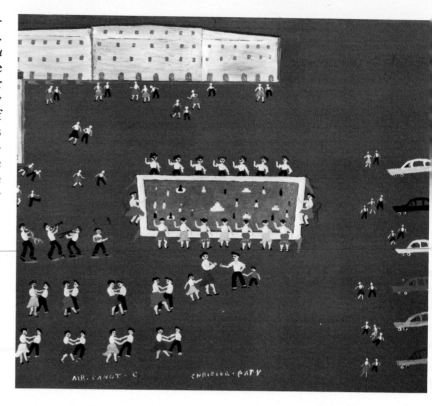

The material rewards of demonic help are believed to be so great that black magic was and is sometimes resorted to, whatever the price to be paid later. Madame de Montespan, the mistress of Louis XIV of France, gave herself over to the terrible rites of black magic, attending ceremonies at which first a goat and then a baby were sacrificed. Her objective was to secure her position as the King's mistress, acquire wealth for herself and her relations, and cause the Queen to be barren.

Today in the West Indies at least one prominent politician is believed to have called in Obeah witchcraft to ensure his success. According to the popular story he sought the advice of the most important Obeah woman in the islands, who assured him that, with her help and in return for a substantial sum, he would achieve his ambition to become a powerful leader. He obeyed her instructions exactly and did in fact achieve his goal, a situation which he quickly used to oust all rivals. But he did not pay the Obeah woman for her services and refused to see her when she called to get her money. She then used her witchcraft to turn his fortune against him. Accidents began to happen to him. He became alarmed and went to her and paid the money he owed. But the Obeah woman said the curse she had put upon him was so strong that, even if she wished to, she would be unable to take it away. Since then accidents of increasing severity have dogged the new leader, who lives in terror.

Right and above: Fertility and prosperity must be encouraged by visual example. Here popular artists play the part of shamans. This coloured woodcut from Vietnam (*right*) shows a hen, well supplied with protein by the insect in her beak, amongst her successfully hatched chicks. Hens play a vital economic role in all poor rural households and are widely used in magic ritual. 'Chrising Paty' by Canute Calyste (*above*), an uneducated native West Indian boat-painter who uses the colours of his job (dark greys, green, maroon, black and white) to paint pictures of subtlety, tenderness and originality. This christening party for his own baby shows how he would have liked it to be (five musicians, six cars, the light-skinned affluence of the white people). (*right*) Colour woodcut on rice-husk paper. 10×8 ins. Traditional; modern example. North Vietnam. Author's collection. (*above*) Canute Calyste. Boat-paint on hardboard. 18×24 ins. Modern. Carriacou, Windward Islands. Author's collection.

Left: The dependence of man on nature is the constant theme of primitive symbolism. Food from the sea, food from the soil, or man cannot himself be fertile and survive. This Polynesian shell-and-seed necklace is a strung prayer that the sea and the soil may continue to supply man with their bounty. *Seeds and shells. Length 36 ins. Traditional. Pago Pago Island, Pacific. Author's collection.*

Right: This foliate paper man from Mexico, vigourously rooting and sprouting, is placed in the fields at the time of sowing. He represents the spirit of vegetation, familiar to us in Europe as the Green Man. Male, he is the active spirit of germination, the end product, the harvest, being symbolized in the female corn dolly.
Paper. Height 10 ins. Traditional; still made. Mexico City. Author's collection.

However rich the soil, favourable the climate, and abundant the harvest, peasants all over the world take nothing for granted, believing the gods could, if offended, send drought, flood, blight or hurricane. Therefore they must show gratitude, make sacrifice, refrain from boasting, and constantly remind the gods of their dependence. At each harvest they make a female figure from ripened grain to keep and revere and remind their gods, until the next harvest. This Balinese 'corn dolly' is plaited in the likeness of a goddess.
Plaited palm-leaf and rice straw. Height 8 ins. Traditional; modern make. Bali, Indonesia. Horniman Museum, London.

As great a leap forward in the history of man as his understanding that the sexual act results in a baby, is the knowledge that planted seeds result in a crop. So fundamental a change is involved in abandoning the nomad hunter's life for the settled agricultural life, that it is not surprising to find farmers the world over cautious, conservative, and superstitious, dependent as they are for their livelihood on natural elements quite outside their own control. They try not to take chances and never fail to show the gods that they depend on a good harvest every year. This is a corn dolly from the Balkans, prepared, like other corn dollies in other countries, as a charm to encourage good harvests. She is dressed like a prosperous local lady.

Oats, silk, lace and ribbon. Height 15 ins. 19th century. Montenegro. Horniman Museum, London.

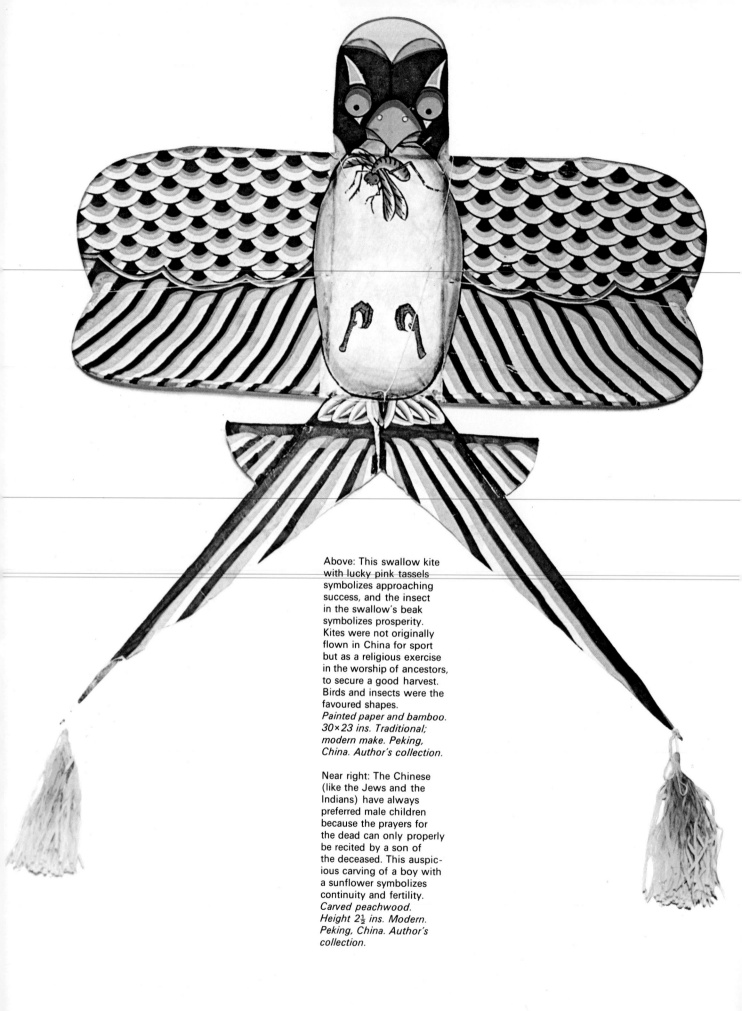

Above: This swallow kite
with lucky pink tassels
symbolizes approaching
success, and the insect
in the swallow's beak
symbolizes prosperity.
Kites were not originally
flown in China for sport
but as a religious exercise
in the worship of ancestors,
to secure a good harvest.
Birds and insects were the
favoured shapes.
*Painted paper and bamboo.
30×23 ins. Traditional;
modern make. Peking,
China. Author's collection.*

Near right: The Chinese
(like the Jews and the
Indians) have always
preferred male children
because the prayers for
the dead can only properly
be recited by a son of
the deceased. This auspicious carving of a boy with
a sunflower symbolizes
continuity and fertility.
*Carved peachwood.
Height 2½ ins. Modern.
Peking, China. Author's
collection.*

Right: The coconut is a symbol of fertility, kept in shrines to be presented to women who want to become mothers, and used in the ritual of wedding ceremonies in India, where today ships are launched by the breaking of a coconut on the bows instead of a bottle of champagne. This perfectly balanced carving was made from three coconuts by an old fisherman, descendant of African slaves, in the Windward Islands. The loving birds, setting up a nest together, are carved from one king coconut and their eyes are seeds. *Coconuts and seeds. Height 8 ins. Modern. Grenada, Windward Islands. Author's collection.*

Right: The cock is the symbol of male virility and its proud comb and splendid tail are popular in folk art. *Painted tin. Height 8 ins. Modern. Acapulco, Mexico. Author's collection.*

Far right: This primitive metal shrine shows a husband and wife magically connected with the arched rainbow of fertility. *Bronze. Height 4 ins. Traditional. India. Author's collection.*

Below: The jug is a symbol of the female. The woman-headed spout of this Mexican jug is moulded into features and jewelled. The jug is painted with magic-protective fertility symbols. A revolving sun, from which shoot growing tendrils ending in spirals, and the Aztec theme of the eagle alighting on a cactus (male and female birds) appear on the front and back of the jug for extra security. The 'neck-lace' is formed of water and wave patterns. The jug is of common ware for daily domestic use in the village.
Painted, unglazed clay. Height 12½ ins. Traditional; still made. Tierra Colorada, Guerrero, West Mexico. Author's collection.

Right: This goat-head mask is used in the Christmas/ New Year revels in the Polish High Tatras. Among the revellers who romp through the snow from cottage to cottage is the Turon, a youth wearing this goat-head symbol of sexuality with spiral curved horns. He chases the girls, catches them and gives them a prickly kiss. The Turon symbolizes the active life-force which is being commanded to return in the spring after the long winter.
Goat-skin, goat horns, coin eyes, string, leather animated jaw. Length 21 ins. Pagan; still used. High Tatras, Poland. Horniman Museum, London.

Right: These realistic wooden figures from the East Indies were prepared for use in magic ritual to assist the safe birth of a child. It is the visual effect of symbols which is vital to their effect. Magic is being seen to be done. The problem and anxiety of childbirth are expressed and resolved.
Carved wood. Height 10 ins. Traditional. Kenyah and Klemantan, Sarawak. British Museum, London.

Left: This common vegetable pounder, bought in a village market in Angola, is the ancient African diabolo shape, signifying male/female. The upper triangle pointing downwards symbolized female sexuality, the lower triangle pointing upwards, male sexuality. In diabolo form they are mutually dependent. Superimposed they indicate sexual union (as in the six-pointed fertility star of Egypt and the Hebrew Star of David). *Carved wood. Height 4½ ins. Traditional; still used. Angola, West Africa. Author's collection.*

Above: Insignia of a witch coven. The triangle crown is the ancient Egyptian phallic potency symbol. The pentangle itself has eight points and thirteen sides, symbolizing the eight ritual occasions and the thirteen lunar months, as well as reincarnation and eternity. *Drawn. Size variable. Pagan origin; widely in use today. English version.*

Left: Feliciano Béjar's modern version of the ancient pagan male-potency symbol, the upward-pointing triangle. *Feliciano Béjar. Iron, glass, metal, screws, eyelets and paper. 5 ft × 26 ins. Modern. Michoacan, Mexico. Béjar collection.*

Above: The ancient diabolo sign of male/female sexuality is used in symbols indicating woman. The symbol on the left is prehistoric, scratched on rock in a recently discovered cave in the Lovo region of the Lower Central Congo. On the right the traditional Sioux sign for woman, which was drawn, cut, sewn or beaded.

Left: Traditional toys are designed not only to amuse the infant but also to scare off evil spirits.
(top to bottom) Tiger rattle. Red-stained palm leaf, small stones inside. Length 5 ins. Traditional design. Madras, India. Humming-bird rattles. Dyed palm-leaf with dried pips. Length 10 ins. Modern design. Grenada, Windward Islands. Toy sword in scabbard. Red varnished cardboard, mirror and glitter. Length 18 ins. Modern. Hong Kong. Teether. Silver, coral, bells, whistle. Length 6 ins. Traditional design; 19th-century example. England. Courtesy of Cameo Corner, London.

Right: This popular Chinese baby-sling magically guards the baby inside. Flowers are lucky; red is auspicious; and the patch is brightly embroidered with characters which mean long life and good fortune or riches and nobility.
Flowered red cotton; patch embroidered with coloured silks. Patch 18 ins. square. Traditional design; used by the poorest people. Modern. Hong Kong.

Right: The legend of Adam and Eve, in infinite variations, is found in every country in the world, fulfilling a universal longing for a fairy-tale past when the world was a garden, animals and vegetation well-disposed, and the only humans loving and innocent.
Dan Jones. Water-colour. 18×21 ins. 1968. London. Author's collection.

Above: The concept of a god of love born in humble circumstances has a particular appeal for the poor, the hungry, the oppressed. The Hindu legend of the birth of Krishna has many similarities to the Christian nativity. Krishna was born amongst animals on a farm where his mother had taken refuge from murderous pursuit. In this toy model the farm elder comes outside the barred entrance to display the holy infant on a winnowing tray to admiring beasts, soldiers and women.
Painted, varnished wood. 12×12 ins. Traditional design. Calcutta, India. Author's collection.

Left: This popular painting from Ethiopia, which establishes the mystique of kingship, describes in sequence the historic journey down the Nile, the famous meeting between King Solomon and the Queen of Sheba, Solomon's dalliance both with Sheba and her handmaid, the two resulting sons, and the subsequent enquiry and judgment to establish the rightful heir, from whom the present Emperor claims direct descent.
Earth colours on coarse canvas. 3×6 ft. Traditional; 1949. Addis Ababa, Ethiopia. Author's collection.

Right: Children, especially boys, need magic protection against jealous demons. Dressing boys as girls is a widespread method of tricking demons. This photograph shows a number of English village boys and girls all dressed as girls—the boys can only be distinguished by their shorter hair.
1890. Hill Wootton, Warwickshire, England.

Above: The *giranta*, the insignia which summons an aboriginal boy of the Central Australian desert to his initiation ordeal. The *giranta* is borne by a messenger who also carries a flaming torch.
Branches, human hair, blood, feathers. Traditional. Central Australia. Adelaide Museum.

Right: These two line-drawings illustrate Aztec playthings made in clay. The one at the top is a rattle, the one at the bottom a whistle. Both are demon-repellent. The pregnant-woman rattle reveals the Mexican obsession with life and death, the demons being warned off the child to come as well.
Red clay. Length: whistle 8 ins; rattle 10 ins. Traditional. Museo Nacionale, Mexico City.

Right: Masks confer magic power on the wearer, power that is enhanced by movement in dancing. In New Guinea magic-protective fertility dance-masks (to encourage and safeguard new life) are sometimes much taller than the dancer inside, reaching twenty-five feet or more. They are hung with boar tusks, horn-bill beaks, feathers and fruit like a magic tree.
8 ft. Middle Sepik, New Guinea. Gallery Primitive, Sydney, Australia.

Below: Bali accepted Hinduism and adapted the ethic to its own art forms. This Balinese dance-mask preaches a moral lesson on the horror of evil. Flaming ears, animal tusks and fangs, protruding eyes, and a travestied third eye symbolize the evil power of this foul demon who will be vanquished by the princely power of good in the dance.

Painted, gilded wood and leather, hair and feathers. Length 28 ins, with trailing feathers which touch the ground. Traditional design; modern make. Bali. Horniman Museum, London.

Left: Traditional Japanese military uniform was designed to terrify the enemy as well as protect and aggrandize the wearer. This so-menpo or iron faceguard was worn in battle by high-ranking officers, to inspire panic in the adversary.

Wrought iron. Height 10 ins. Traditional, worn until 1870; worn today ceremonially. Japan. Horniman Museum, London.

Below: This dance-mask from the Congo is the insignia of a secret society, an essential part of the regalia used in magic ceremonies to promote fertility or destruction. Such masks are often worn with an attached hanging of raffia to conceal the dancer's body. The dance-masks of West Africa rank amongst the most powerful works of art in the world. The deep religious awe which inspired them, no less than the amazingly skilled use of unlikely materials, sets them in a category of their own.

Painted wood, feathers. Traditional. Congo. Horniman Museum, London.

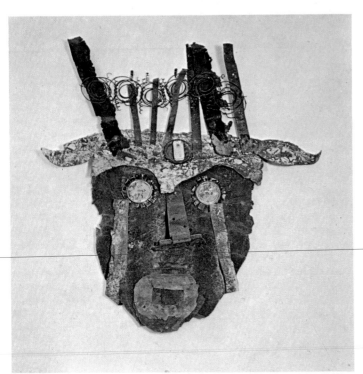

Above and right top: Two masks by a young Englishman, Dan Jones, who knows West Africa. Put together from rusty tins, broken bolts and corroded bedsprings, the rust imparts a strange patina. *Above:* Evil Spirit. *Top right:* Good Spirit. *Dan Jones. Tin, bedsprings, hinges. Height 3 ft. 1968. England. Author's collection.*

Right: This horrific modern dance-mask from Bolivia, with its mirrors, spiral horns, toothed wings, protruding eyes and reptiles symbolizes and denounces the evil usage of precious metals. It is worn by Bolivian Indian miners when they dance *La Diablada* to celebrate the feast day of the Virgin of Socavon, whose shrine is near the Oruro mines. *Lacquered papier-maché, electric-light bulbs, rubber, mirrors. Height 3 ft. Oruro, Bolivia. Modern. Horniman Museum, London.*

Right: This large fish with a baby fish (or perhaps its prey) is a symbol of good luck, hung outside a booth in Tunisia as a shopsign to attract and increase prosperity. The colour of the Prophet Mohammed (green) and the glittering sequins repel demons, and the fringe is rain-inducing. *Black cloth, beads, sequins, embroidery, fringe. Length 36 ins. Modern. Tunisia. Dr Otto Samson collection.*

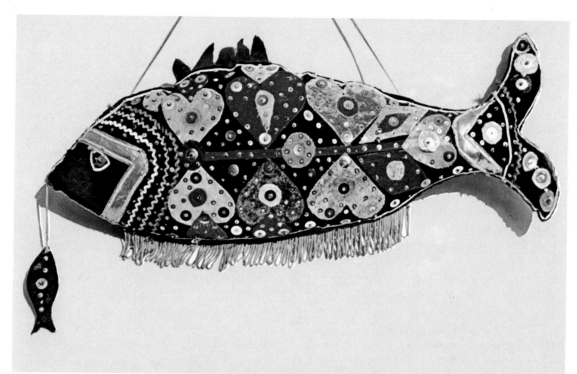

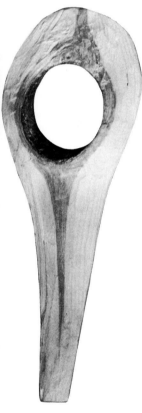

Above: Wooden charm used by Polish peasants to relieve a cow of the evil spirits which upset her milk yield. The cow watches while her milk is ritually poured through the hole of the 'cow-unbewitcher' with appropriate incantations. The shape of this implement incorporates both male and female symbols. Charms to protect milk and butter are very widespread. *Carved wood. Length 8 ins. Traditional; possibly still used in rural Poland. Horniman Museum, London.*

A ship is also a dwelling, more dangerous to occupy than a house and needing strong magic protection. This the figurehead, the soul of the vessel, supplied. Even after the age of steam had begun both Royal Navy and mercantile ships clung to their adored, brilliantly painted and gilded figureheads. These cigarette cards show figureheads from famous fighting ships. *Carved, painted wood. Size variable. Traditional; examples from 18th and 19th centuries. British Royal Navy*

Left and right: In all dry countries it is the women who are the water-carriers, perhaps because water is a female element. Even little girls must learn how to balance water-pots on their heads. To hold the vessel steady, a padded head-ring is worn. Since it comes in close contact with the vulnerable head and the vital water, this head-ring needs strong magic protection against ill-intentioned demons. In India, as in Africa, cowrie shells are lucky symbols of fertility and wealth. Further protection is offered by tassels and fringes, symbolizing welcome rain, and by powerful demon-repellent mirrors (left).
(left) Padded cotton, cowrie shells, mirrors, tassels. Length approx. 20 ins. Modern. India. Horniman Museum, London.
(right) Padded cotton, cowrie shells. Length 30 ins. Modern. Kathiawar. India. Horniman Museum, London.

Left: This early sewing machine was intended for ladies of leisure to use as a drawing-room pastime. It is elegantly ornamented with lucky spirals and magic-protective gold borders in meander, cloud, and rayed-sun repeat patterns. It stands on five-clawed guardian-animal feet.
Iron and steel, porcelain handle; gilt and mother-of-pearl ornament. Length 17 ins. 1850. England. Author's collection.

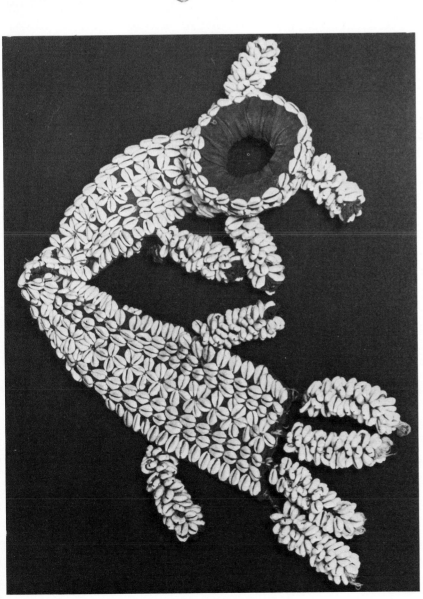

Top: This toy elephant is decorated like a live elephant on ceremonial occasions, with growing-plant symbols, 'eyes of god', lucky spirals and protective magic borders. The elephant is sacred both to Hindus and Buddhists. The Hindu elephant deity Ganesha, adored as the remover of obstacles, presides over the cardinal points, standing on the back of a tortoise to support the world. Particularly is the white elephant, bringer of rain and fertility.
Painted papier-mâché. Height 12 ins. Modern. Bombay, India. Author's collection.

Above: Haircomb in the shape of a lucky elephant, sacred to Buddhism as one of the seven holy treasures. The three-toed white elephant is worshipped as causing the magic impregnation of Maya, immaculate mother of Buddha.
Tortoise-shell comb. Length 8¼ ins. Modern. Ceylon. Author's collection.

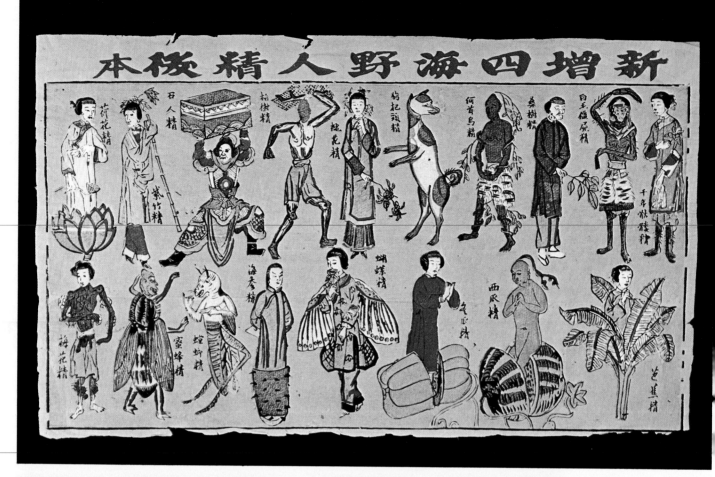

Above: Popular Chinese
print listing 'the big
collection of barbaric evil
spirits within the realm'.
Reading left to right (*top*):
the evil spirits of lotus,
bamboo, stone sculpture,
fir tree, peach tree, dog,
willow tree, mulberry tree,
vampire, 1000-year-old
dead man; (*bottom*) plum
tree, honey-bee, grass-
hopper, sea-cucumber,
butterfly, winter melon,
water melon, banana tree.
Chinese print. 11½ × 20 ins.
Traditional. Hong Kong.
Author's collection.

Left: Red is the Chinese
colour of good fortune.
This red printed cotton
twill celebrated the first
Russian sputnik and was
issued when relations
between the two countries
were more cordial.
Arriving in a Chinese
heaven, the sputnik is
greeted by Chinese apsaras
extending their polite
patronage.
Printed red twill. 1960.
Peking, China. Author's
collection.

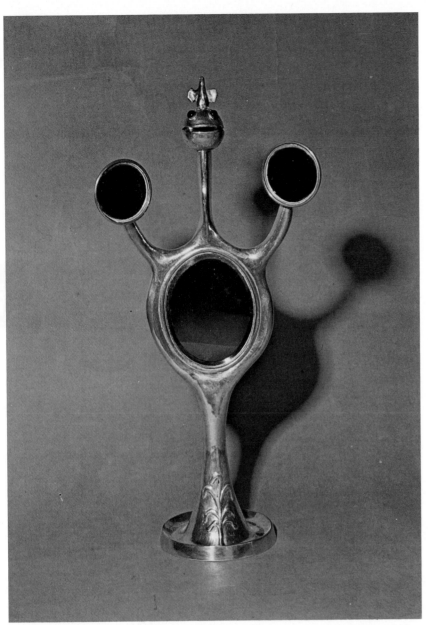

Left: Animism knows no national frontiers. This triple-mirrored garnet-eyed creature, whose mouth opens to take in and safeguard rings, is the creation of the late Polish-Jewish poet-jeweller, Mosheh Oved. It might have come out of Africa or Mexico. But it was designed and cast in the heart of London.
Silver, garnets, mirrors. Height 24 ins. Modern. Cameo Corner, London.

Left: This vegetable-cutter in the form of a guardian animal with food in its mouth prevents demons from interfering with the food. India, with its very ancient religions and magic taboos, is extremely pollution-conscious. What may be eaten and how, how food may be prepared and by whom, all form a considerable part of the trauma of Indian life, from the highest to the lowest caste, and from palaces to village everyday life. The concern is not only who may prepare food and how, but with what. Every implement touching food must be heavily guarded by magic protective rituals and safeguards lest evil spirits creep in and do mischief.
Iron. Height 10 ins. 19th century. India. Horniman Museum, London.

Above: This bee-hive is shaped into a devil mask, with jutting tongue and staring glass eyes. Peasants not only decorate their own dwellings with magic-protective devices against intruding evil spirits, but they see that their livestock is no less carefully protected. Especially rich in this branch of popular art are Poland and Slovakia, where sheep-pens, hen-houses, byres, dog-kennels and bee-hives are lavishly adorned with brightly-painted anti-demonic symbols.
Straw overlaid with clay and painted, glass eyes. Variable size. 19th century. Prievidza, Central Slovakia. Slovak National Museum.

Above: Dance-mask from Orissa portraying Shiva, the destroyer and potent regenerator, whose third eye once saved the world from darkness and can also reduce wrong-doers to ashes in a flash. Note the serpent head-dress, in which rests Gunga (the river Ganges), replenishing her fertility in his hair on her way to earth.
Painted papier-maché. 12×12 ins. Traditional design; modern make. Orissa, India. Author's collection.

Right: The Eye of Horus, from the inside of an Egyptian mummy-case where it was painted to guard the dead from harm. There are good ways of using eyes and evil ways. Good include the blessing received by looking at a holy object or successful person (*darsan*); bad, and very common, the curse received from a malevolent person with the evil eye.
Moulded painted clay. Ancient Egypt.

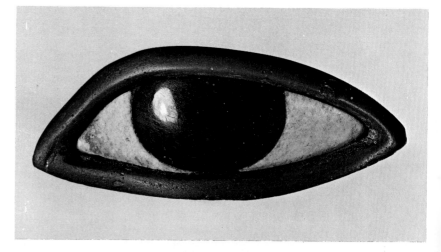

Above: Head of Bodhisattava, a saint on the way to attaining celestial bliss. The third eye or *urna* in the centre of the forehead is not the terrible third eye of Shiva the destroyer but the gentle Buddhist third eye of spiritual wisdom, and in this small bronze it is indented so that it can contain a jewel.
Bronze. Height 6 ins. Traditional design; modern make. North India, near Tibet. Author's collection.

Above: Portuguese fishing boat with eyes painted on its prow. Boats need eyes to find their way over the sea; fishing boats need eyes to locate the shoals of fish; sailors in the boats need magic protection against danger and bad luck. For thousands of years ships and boats in the Orient have been painted with magic-protective eyes. Today Chinese junks continue this ancient practice. The Hindu 'eye-bestowal' rite is the ritual chiselling of the eye of a statute, preceded by meditation and prayer. It is the act which completes the idol and establishes its power. This practice also exists in China, where even today the parade dragon is ritually 'enlivened' by the painting in of its eyes (preferably by someone of distinction or high rank) before it can be animated.
Paint. Variable size. Traditional; still used. Portugal; and many Eastern countries.

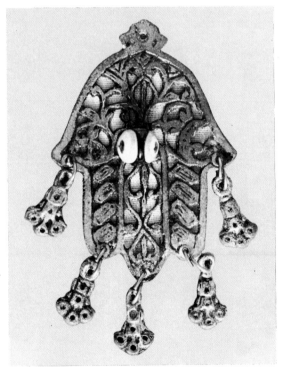

Above: The Hand of Fatimah, an Arab talismanic pendant with power to repel the evil eye. Fatimah was the wife of the Prophet Mohammed. Her hand arrests the evil eye. Reinforcement is provided by the double ceramic eye on the palm of the hand; this catapults the curse back on the sender.
Lead with ceramic eye. Length 3 ins. Traditional design; modern make. Arab; Jerusalem. Author's collection.

When Harriet, the old gypsy queen, died, her caravan with its cherished contents (pots and pans, white lace shawls, brass candlesticks, etc.) was burned in accordance with gypsy tradition, and both her horses were shot. For Harriet's spirit needed her possessions in the next world. Her body was buried in the local churchyard, to be remembered with flowers when her family passed that way on their endless migrations. No-one should be sent off to the spirit world without belongings for the spirit is angered by such shabby treatment.

Death and after-life

Appeasing the dead

Primitive peoples believe that, however humble in life, once a man or woman is dead, the spirit immediately becomes powerful and potentially dangerous. For then it is free to wander and, if it feels like being spiteful, can injure the crops, prevent rain falling, send plagues and barrenness to the living. Ancestors, as they recede in time, become more and more powerful until finally they are worshipped as gods. The elaborate and costly funerals of China, India and Mexico are based on the fear that if the dead person's spirit is not satisfied with the honours accorded in death it will return to wreak vengeance on the living.

With the raising of standards of living and education, the primitive preoccupation with spirits and their appeasement lessens, turning into superstition and finally into a kind of uneasy joke. The Chinese no longer believe that any noise in the night is the malevolent call of a hungry spirit and hurry to burn paper money outside the house to solace it by attention. But in England many rational well-educated people still shiver when they hear an owl hoot in the night, are uneasy when they break a mirror, and are careful to insert an annual remembrance of their dead parents in *The Times*. It is considered wrong to 'speak ill of the dead', and total strangers raise their hats as a funeral passes by in the streets of London. Why? It is customary and would be ill-mannered not to do so, they say. But there is a more sinister reason behind these customs. 'Our dead are never dead to us until we have forgotten them. They can be injured by us. They can be wounded. And the aged peasant-woman most of all believes that her dead are conscious.' Thus wrote George Eliot of nineteenth-century England.

The Hindu funeral ceremony clearly demonstrates a lively fear of the dead. Sacred verses are first recited to revive the person, if life is still there. When this fails the priest announces the death, which signals the immediate outburst of great noise. Professional mourners tear their hair and shriek rhythmically, noise being essential to frighten off evil spirits.

Not only the Hindus believe that loud noises scare off evil spirits. Richard Henry Dana describes (in *Two Years before the Mast*) how in 1835, ashore in the Californian port of Santa Barbara, he attended the Roman Catholic funeral of a little girl: 'The most singular thing of all was that two men walked, one on either side of the coffin, carrying muskets in their hands which they continually fired into the air. Whether this was to keep off the evil spirits or not I do not know. It was the only interpretation I would

put upon it.' In 1970 during the state mourning and funeral of President Nasser of Egypt, rifle-shots were fired at the sky without pause and there was a continual loud wailing. (Conversely, a sure way of getting a prayer safely to the spirit to whom it was addressed was to have it written on paper and then burnt, the odour reaching the region of the intended recipient who could smell the message.)

In a Hindu funeral the corpse is washed, dressed and adorned with jewels. Then the big toes are tied together, and the two thumbs are tied similarly. This is to prevent the ghost of the corpse from returning. The plank of wood dragged after the bier has a similar purpose. With the body auspiciously facing south, the mourners circle the bier anti-clockwise, for they are concerned not with life but with death. With the costliest ceremonies the family can afford, the corpse is then cremated. These rites are assisted by the eldest son, who strews the ashes in a sacred river. The reason for cremation is that so long as a physical body exists Hindus believe the soul will linger near it and be unable to take flight into the new body into which it will be reincarnated. During the funeral, ritual *mantras* carefully direct the various parts of the body to their spirit homes: the eyes to the sun, the vital breath to the atmosphere, the thoughts to the moon, the ear to heaven and the body to earth, the ego to the ether, the head and hair to the plants and the trees, and the blood and seed to the waters. Yet despite all these precautions, the spirits and the ghosts of the dead are believed to be still flying about, seeking to re-enter their former lives. These spirits are more active and malevolent on certain dates, especially the dark half of the month of September/October, when children in particular must be specially protected from them. In order to appease both kindly and evil spirits some Hindu householders place food-offerings out daily for them, on the ground for the kindly spirits and in the dustbin for the evil spirits.

Great efforts are made in many countries to keep the spirit from returning to harry its relations, especially in the dangerous period of the funeral procession and the next few days: by shouting and loud wailing; by moving very slowly and deviously by unknown paths (Haiti); by dropping alternate pebbles to distract and delay the ghost (India); by stopping the orifices of the Emperor's corpse with auspicious jade (Imperial China); and by stopping the corpse's mouth with glass beads and putting hen's eggs and needles in its armpits and in the palms of its hands (Malaya).

Post-missionary demon-scarer from the Indian Ocean (see an earlier version on page 17). The strange white priests also suffered from trouble with demons and they offered the Christian angel as a more powerful anti-demon prophylactic. The new demon-chasers had wings, blue eyes (which could emit lightning) and, like the white priests, attached magic importance to covering the genitals and the head. The white man's top hat was, to the Eastern mind, the symbol of his power and importance. This 19th-century middle-class status symbol (so totally impractical in the torrid tropics) made the strongest impression in India, Africa and China where it was invariably used almost like a physical attribute in native art depicting white men. It seemed proper therefore that the guardian angel should wear this magic crown.
Wood. Height 3 ft. 1887. Nicobar Islands. British Museum, London.

In all countries the execution of criminals has always been attended by terror of what might happen afterwards. It was once customary for the executioner to beg forgiveness of his victim before the execution.

There is an ancient, persistent terror of dying incomplete. The loss of a hand, arm, leg or even an appendix (by accident or amputation) is a disaster in the hereafter, because an incomplete corpse can have no proper spirit life. The Jews and the Chinese had a particular terror of this. Worst of all evils was decapitation, which gave the spirit of the victim no hope at all in the next world. The worst of all crimes to Confucian Chinese was the unfilial behaviour of a son, whose bad conduct so distressed his parents that they committed suicide. The punishment for the son was decapitation, nicely calculated to avenge the outraged spirits of the dead parents, for the headless spirit of their son could receive no recognition nor mercy in the spirit world. Murderers in every country must expect no forgiveness in this world nor the next, and this is why in the East soldiers cut off the head or foot of those they have killed, to keep their ghosts from wandering and making trouble.

So essential was the entirety of a corpse that well-to-do Chinese took care to track down the severed heads of their friends and relations after battle in order to have them sewn back into their rightful bodies before burial, thus giving them a chance of survival in the spirit world. As much as 600 dollars has been recorded as purchase price for such heads.

In Haiti they believe in a female demon named Bocor who captures the souls of corpses, leaving them powerless spirits named 'zombies' which perform the evil Bocor requires of them. Because of this terror of becoming zombies, the dead are often shot or poisoned to make sure that Bocor cannot get at them. Rattles are used and magic incantations are performed by the presiding priest, who crawls inside the pall of the corpse to perform his service. An imposing funeral is held and then a wake, so that the soul of the dead may depart without rancour and not try to return, when Bocor might seize it. Burial takes place before dawn and the coffin is taken to the cemetery by a devious route and buried in as stylish a manner as can be afforded. Some of the most imposing tombs look like splendid houses ornamented with magnificent iron scrollwork. The poor use conches to border their graves, the open ends pointing skyward so that the soul may quickly ascend and be gone.

The Australian aborigines, with their acute sense of the spirit world, had their own method of appeasing spirits. Daisy Bates, a grazier with a great sympathy for the aboriginal peoples, recorded the desert aborigines lighting a spirit fire every evening, south-east of their shelters and inside a low semicircle of bushes, the opening of which also faced south-east. This spirit fire was to comfort the spirits of the recently dead, whose home was north-east, and thus intercept them and keep them from straying into the shelters.

In Nigeria if a Yoruba chief became unpopular, his council sent him an *igbava*, a notice to quit in the shape of a covered cup containing parrot's eggs, a signal that he was expected to commit suicide. If the chief refused to obey this request, the council arranged for him to be strangled, so that no royal blood should be shed, and elected one of his sons to be his successor. Shedding royal blood is always magically dangerous. Marco Polo recorded the execution of a rebel of royal blood in China who was rolled and suffocated in rugs to avoid bringing misfortune on those who survived him.

In China a valuable jewel was placed in the mouth of a corpse, to pay homage to its spirit and so to prevent it from taking offence and wandering about balefully. The type of jewel was ordered strictly according to the rank of the dead person. Jade was placed in the mouth of a mandarin, pearl and gold for less exalted officials, down to three copper cash for common folk.

When a peasant died three kinds of grain were placed in his mouth. This was so that the corpse's spirit would be sure to use its influence to make the crops grow. Chinese fields are dotted with small conical mounds which mark the graves of peasants and which are carefully avoided when the ground is ploughed and sown.

Besides a good suit of clothes and fine pair of shoes, bed and bedding, a house, horses and money were also buried with the corpse, so that its spirit should be comfortable and enjoy status in the next world. The frontier tribes of north-east India and the gypsies have a similar tradition. When a gypsy dies his caravan is burned so that he will have a shelter in the hereafter. Chinese burials were always costly and could be ruinous, because even the poorest survivors were prepared to spend more than they could afford rather than risk angering the spirit of the dead relation they were burying. In the course of time paper effigies of the dead person's effects and wealth were substituted for the real articles and ceremoniously burned at his funeral. This custom survives in Hong Kong, where paper motorcars, paper bungalows, and large amounts of paper 'money' are burned in the street outside the former residence of the deceased.

The coffin remained in the home of the deceased for 100 days of formal family mourning. During this period the sorrowing relations ate with their fingers the food brought in by neighbours and sat and slept on the floor, as no cooking was permitted, nor the use of chopsticks, chairs nor beds. All this devotion was intended to prevent the spirit of the dead relation feeling slighted. Until the best burial site had finally been chosen, the coffin, after the regulation 100 days, was removed to a house in the City of the Dead, where it might remain for months or even years, behind a large screen set between it and the door to prevent the impatient spirit wandering.

Sensitive as they are to the power of their ancestors, and punctilious as they are in omitting nothing which may comfort and please the dead, the Chinese have evolved a remarkable two-way process in their filial piety. This is a magic power they call *fengshui*. By this magic, wind and water can be coaxed to act for the benefit of people who behave with virtue towards their ancestors.

It is vital that dead parents should be buried in the most geomantically favourable site—that is where wind, water and mountains combine to make the dead happy and comfortable—so that their spirits will be aware of these honours and gratefully bring good crops, good business and general good luck to the family. A geomancer is employed to decide on the best site to attract favourable juxtaposition of the cosmic *yin* and *yang* breath. The heights and forms of the land and buildings on the land influence this breath, according to calculable magic rules ascertained by use of dowsing rod and astrological compass.

It is also possible, with the help of talismans and charms, to modify the dangers of unpropitious burial sites where the *status quo* might be altered by the construction of new roads, bridges or buildings. Railways and tunnels (dangerous because straight and therefore demon-favoured) are always unpropitious. When Hong Kong's College of Chung Chi was expanded the re-sited villagers refused to move into their new houses because the geomancer declared the *fengshui* unfavourable: the front roof-pitch of each house was shorter than that at the back, and this would have caused later generations to dwindle in prosperity. The solution, discovered in learned texts, was to paint all the roof beams auspicious red, so geomantically reversing the bad luck.

Feng-shui was codified by Kuo P'o, a student who died in AD 324, and the scholar Wang Chi, of the Sung dynasty, who wrote: 'For a grave, a wide river in front, a high cliff behind, with enclosing hills to the right and left, would constitute a first-class geomantic position. Houses and graves face the south, because the annual animation of the vegetable kingdom with the approach of summer comes from that quarter; the deadly influences of winter come from the north.'

The protective roof-top images, the protective door-god prints, and the guardian stone images before important tombs are all there in order to generate favourable *feng-shui*, not only for the family concerned but for the whole locality. Since belief in *feng-shui* covered the whole of China, even the dry flat north where rivers and mountains are absent, the geomancers had to make continual accommodations. In a flat desert, for instance, the slightest mound could take the place of the necessary mountain. *Feng-shui* is still practised in Hong Kong, where Western-educated professors, sceptical of all other forms of magic, still call in the geomancer before building a house or buying a burial-place for their family.

Simple people think that if grandmother is comfortable and happy with the site selected by the geomancer she will be pleased with her living relations, who have tried to see to her comfort, 'her bones will glow', and in return for their thoughtfulness she will exert herself from the spirit world to see that her grandchildren pass their examinations, that her son's business makes a good profit, and that her descendants will be lucky in their undertakings. The obligation is mutual. The legendary Hou Hao declared: 'If ghosts are careful to repay a kindness, surely live men should do the same.'

The Ch'ing Ming festival, in April every year, celebrates the care of the dead by their living relations, who gather at the grave with brooms and hoes to clear away the weeds and make the site clean and tidy, and also bring with them trays of food to share with the dead, incense-sticks to please their spirit nostrils and fire-crackers to chase away demons. Gold and silver paper is ceremoniously burned and paper money is offered. When the ceremony is over, slips of lucky red and white paper, like streamers, are fastened to the corners of the grave as proof that the ritual has been duly observed. In Hong Kong Ch'ing Ming is still meticulously celebrated and factories and workshops are closed for the day.

Even the Emperor of China himself was not immune to the threat from aggrieved spirits. Each year he was obliged to walk, clad in penitential garments, from the Hall of Fasting to the Altar of Heaven, where, with ritual kowtowing, he implored the gods to forgive any unjust or mistaken executions carried out during the previous year.

The spirits of those who died in wars or famine, or who had no living relations to

Tibetan spirit trap, fastened on the house-roof after being given authorization and magic power in a ritual-prayer by the shaman, a prophylactic against demons approaching from the sky. Like the Hindu kolem this spirit trap is fashioned into a symmetrical design of occult significance. The wilder, the more difficult to inhabit a country is, the more powerful and exaggerated must be the counteracting magic protection. In Tibet, where human beings have had to come to terms with terrifying natural conditions, they have kept down their population (essential where so little food is available) by polyandry and by sending large numbers of men and women into monasteries and nunneries, where (released from undesired breeding) they engage in continual magic ritual to appease powerful gods and defy demons. Tibetan religious teachers have developed extraordinary spiritual/physical controls: walking so rapidly it looks like flying, immunity to freezing and burning, telepathic communication, etc.
Wood, straw, string and animal skull. Length 26 ins. Traditional; possibly now discouraged by Chinese administrators. Dr Otto Samson collection.

sacrifice for them, also had to be appeased, and regular public subscriptions were organized to pay for prayers for them; these prayers were preceded by processions of priests bearing lanterns and torches and beating gongs. So that no lurking demons should interfere with the efficacy of the prayers offered, red candles were lit in every corner and beside every bridge. The authorities also prudently ordered a great festival for the dead every ten years. A huge image of Yama, the terrible god of death, was set up in every temple courtyard, before which were burned immense quantities of paper clothes, paper money, paper spectacles, paper food, paper transport, even paper opium pipes, so that not a single neglected spirit might not be so reached and appeased.

In Mexico, the Day of the Dead gathers families at the graves of their ancestors, where they share as sumptuous a feast as they can afford and burn candles in candelabra representing the tree of life.

In Arab countries families visit the ancestral grave for a picnic as a pleasurable duty.

In Europe and America, Hallowe'en is the festival when the dead must be appeased and made much of, so that they will consent to lie quiet the rest of the year. It is a time when witches are about and great bonfires are traditionally set blazing to frighten them off. Guy Fawkes' Day (5 November) has taken over the bonfire ceremony from Hallowe'en in Great Britain.

Conjuring up spirits

Despite the universal terror of the spirits of the dead, all countries have techniques for getting in touch with them. Dancing and drumming to induce a tranced state, through which the spirit invoked will speak, is basic to every magic religion. It was and is practised in Tahiti, in Mexico, in Bali, in Haiti, in North America, and in Europe. Today's spiritualist groups in England are nervously putting their toes on to a long-established and well-prepared road.

Voodoo is the magic religion of Haiti. The voodoo séance begins by the marking of the circle and the drawing of the *vévé* round a decorated central post. This design is the earthly representation of the spirit which is to be invoked. When summoned, the spirit will slip down the post and go to its *vévé*. At every séance the *vévé* is destroyed during the dancing; like all special magic, its power only works once. Next candles are lit and water is sprinkled on the ground. Then the drumming and dancing begin. The spirit *loa* is begged to descend and make itself heard through the imploring medium's

This spirit dance-mask was used by shamans of the Kwakiutl tribe of Canadian Indians in what is now British Columbia. Protected between the Pacific Ocean and the Rocky Mountains, which supplied them with salmon and bear-meat, the West Canadian Indian tribes achieved an impressive economic/artistic culture, based on totemism (their totem poles are famous), the Potlach, and spirit possession.
Painted wood. Height 11 ins. 19th century. Kwakiutl tribe; Canada. Horniman Museum, London.

body. Then a blood sacrifice is offered: a chicken, a goat, or even a bull. The drumming and dancing increase in tempo and there is vigorous falsetto chanting from the attending priests and priestesses, to keep out unwanted spirits. As in Shango-Baptist séances, trance is induced by varying the drumming rhythms. Professional drummers direct their drumming particularly towards those who are showing signs of falling into trance. Finally these dancers are toppled off into true trance by a rattling tempo on the *shakkas*.

The devotee in a trance acts like one possessed, eyes staring and the voice of the *loa* coming out of her in a strange sound not her own, answering questions and giving advice. This trance may last hours or days, and when the woman recovers herself she has no memory at all of what has happened.

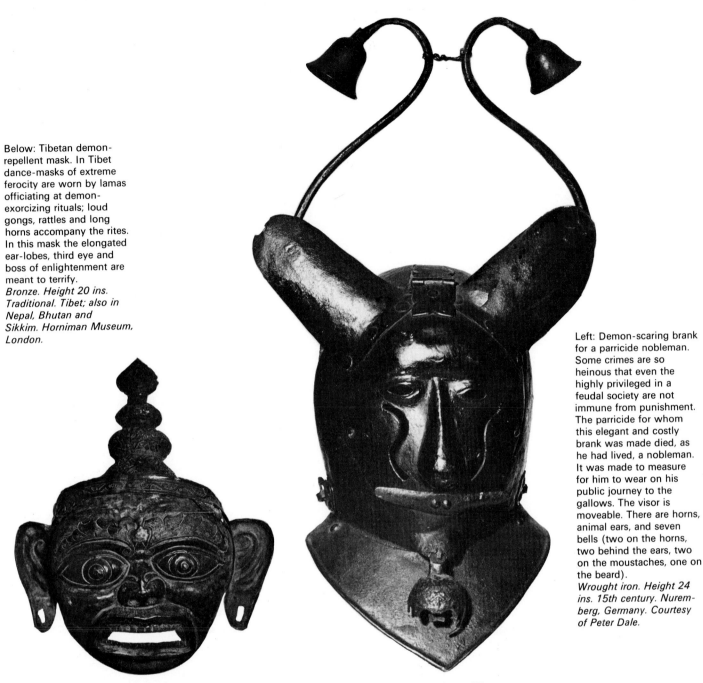

Below: Tibetan demon-repellent mask. In Tibet dance-masks of extreme ferocity are worn by lamas officiating at demon-exorcizing rituals; loud gongs, rattles and long horns accompany the rites. In this mask the elongated ear-lobes, third eye and boss of enlightenment are meant to terrify. *Bronze. Height 20 ins. Traditional. Tibet; also in Nepal, Bhutan and Sikkim. Horniman Museum, London.*

Left: Demon-scaring brank for a parricide nobleman. Some crimes are so heinous that even the highly privileged in a feudal society are not immune from punishment. The parricide for whom this elegant and costly brank was made died, as he had lived, a nobleman. It was made to measure for him to wear on his public journey to the gallows. The visor is moveable. There are horns, animal ears, and seven bells (two on the horns, two behind the ears, two on the moustaches, one on the beard). *Wrought iron. Height 24 ins. 15th century. Nuremberg, Germany. Courtesy of Peter Dale.*

Voodoo is often used, like all black magic, to obtain wealth at another's expense. As the participants are dealing with the dangerous spirits of the dead, whom they are never sure of being able to control, voodoo cults are shot with fear and terror. One voodoo ritual is designed to transfer the talents of a dead man to a living man, the gift being usually of a professional nature, such as a lawyer or doctor.

All over the world the conjuring of demons is always a dangerous procedure, for it might succeed only too well. As all the demons are believed to be hovering anxiously within range, waiting their opportunity to force their way into human affairs, every evocation is attended by risk. All the official magic manuals (and many have been published) dwell on the danger, especially in black magic ritual, of attracting unwanted, uncalled-for demons, who will not go away once they have succeeded in getting into the magic circle.

After the instruments have been prepared, the correct magic circle drawn and the incantations delivered, the summoner of the particular demon required must quickly establish power over it. In black magic ritual this is the key to all the procedure. The demon will delay and prevaricate until threatened and bullied into submission. The purpose for which the demon has been summoned must be explained and the demon must be forced to comply. Then it has to be dismissed as brutally as it was summoned. This is regarded as the most difficult part of the ceremony. It will try every trick to stay inside the ring and may even try to slip in demon associates, who will be anxiously crowding outside the magic circle.

Left and far left: Two objects from totally different societies express the same deep desire for spirit guidance and protection. One is a sophisticated religious papercut made by a Polish peasant to protect her cottage, the other a hunting club made and used by an Australian desert aborigine to kill the day's food. However poor, the Polish peasant lives in an integrated lively community with a beautiful church full of images and a well-stocked village market, and she has a rich pagan-pastoral tradition to inform her imagination. But the two world wars which so changed the face of Europe have decimated her family and left terrible scars on her village. She needs security and her papercut pleads for fertility and continuity. The Australian desert aborigine who laboriously cut and shaped this club must hunt every day. The emu, his prey, runs very fast and most days he catches nothing. The club is pocked into a spirit path, growing from a female, on which stand nine emus, his dream of the game he must catch if his skeletal family is to survive.
(left) Wood. Length 19 ins. Modern. Central deserts, Australia.
(far left) Antonina Staskewicz. Paper. Height 9½ ins. Modern. Poland.

Above: Extreme emotional stress can activate spirit-writing in ordinary people. Madge Gill, an East End housewife who died in 1961 aged 77, began to pour out extraordinary drawings—some being thirty feet long—after the death of a beloved son. She believed herself directed by a spirit named Myrninerest.
Madge Gill. Ink on post-card. 1955. London.

Right: A vévé is an occult signature diagram drawn on the ground in corn gruel or ashes at voodoo ceremonies to summon the desired *loa* (god). The *loa* descends into the séance down a striped central pole, round which the vévé is drawn. A few examples (*top to bottom*): vévés for Agwé, god of the sea, Erzulie, goddess of luxurious and tragic love, Avizan, goddess of spirit protection, and Ghede, guardian god of the dead. Vévés are sprinkled with food offerings and destroyed during the séance, being newly drawn each time. From 1510 onwards slaves from the West African coast took their drums and magic cults with them to Haiti, where they joined Carribean magic cults, resulting in voodoo (voudoun). Today voodoo also shows French influences, in the character of the *loa* Baron Samedi for instance.
Wheatflour, maize or ashes. Size variable. Modern. Haiti and West Indies.

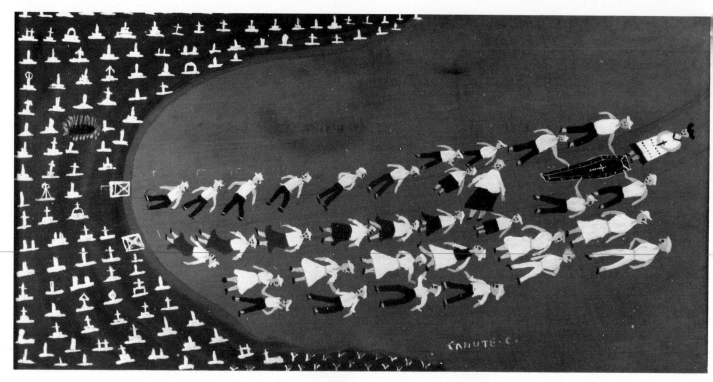

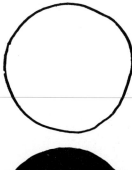

Above: A funeral procession seen through the eyes of Canute Calyste, a West Indian boat-painter. This painting gives an extraordinary sensation of phallic action and exploding energy, of life triumphing over death. *Canute Calyste. Boat-paint on wood. 32×17 ins. Modern. Carriacou, Windward Islands. Author's collection.*

Right: This modern ceramic tile by Peggy Angus has the same clarity and directness as the Sioux sign-writing. It invokes night/day, hate/love and death/life. *Peggy Angus. Glazed ceramic. 6 ins. square. Modern. London. Author's collection.*

Above: The Sioux sign-writing for (*top to bottom*) life, death and eternity. *Scratched on bark, animal skin or rocks. Traditional. Sioux tribe; Dakota, United States.*

Right: A 19th-century engraving of supernatural terror. This horrific drawing by the French artist Grandville belongs to the post-Byronic romantic melancholy era. Grandville's haunted excursions into the everyday supernatural probably influenced Tenniel in his *Alice in Wonderland* drawings, and certainly inspired the French surrealists in the 20th century. *Grandville (J. I. I. Gérard). Pen drawing from 'Petites Misères de la Vie Humaine'. 10½×6½ ins. 1835. Paris.*

Above: The resurrection of Christ and of nature are celebrated in every Polish village by lavish egg decoration, new papercuts, new domestic wall-decoration over new white-wash, new sand-pictures on earth floors. This lovely resurrection chandelier is made from what else-where would be discarded as debris.
Straw, painted egg-shells, paper flowers and cut-outs. 3×3 ft. 19th century. Poland. Horniman Museum, London.

Right: Tree-fibre mat from Domenica. The fish symbolizes fecundity and resurrection throughout the world because of its association with life-giving water.
Tree fibre, sewn by hand. Length 28 ins. Modern. Domenica. Author's collection.

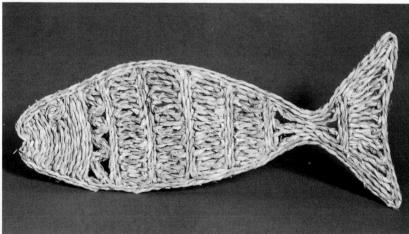

Left: This austere and touching gravepost stands sentinel over a peasant's grave in Vietnam, where the peacock is the symbol of resurrection.
Carved wood. Height 6 ft. Traditional. Vietnam. Horniman Museum, London.

Right: In European folklore the swan is the symbol of death because it is usually seen swimming, reflected in reverse in water. Whatever dies, in popular thought, must be reborn. Therefore it has long been the custom in European domestic ornament, where the swan continues to be popular, to associate it with evergreen plants. In the 19th century ceramic swans were planted with an aspidistra and placed in the parlour window or filled with eggs and put in the windows of dairies. Either way they were a symbol of resurrection.
White ceramic. 12 × 17½ ins. Traditional. England. Author's collection.

Bottom right: The hope of life after death is often the solace of the bereaved. Somewhere beyond the far-off sky they dream of being united at last and forever with the one they have lost. This anguished pen-drawing reveals such a yearning.
Madge Gill. Ink-drawing on postcard. Modern. England. Author's collection.

Above: This motorized
Singapore funeral bier,
gorgeously decorated with
silk and paper butterflies,
lanterns, flowers, fringes,
tassels, spirals, roof-animals
and dragons, is intended
to please and pacify the
spirit of the departed.
*Silk and paper. Modern.
Singapore.*

Below: Australian desert
aborigine *kaidiche*, executioner's slippers, could only
be worn once. The print of
their emu-feather soles
was a death-sentence to
the wrongdoer, who
recognized this judgment,
knew himself to be a non-
person, sickened and died.
*Human hair, emu feathers.
Length 8 ins. Traditional.
Central deserts, Australia.*

Right: Death sentence for
children in a Nazi concentration camp, painted by
a self taught artist who
survived such a camp.
*Perle Hessing. Oils on board.
22×30 ins. Modern. London.*

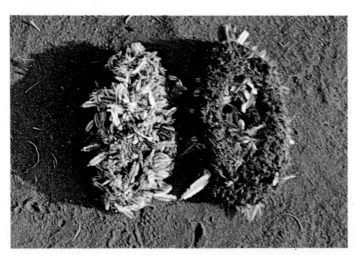

Left: Mexican tree of life, decorated with children, birds (heavenly messengers), flowers and angels; others include God the Father. It is taken to the cemetery on the Day of the Dead, and its candles are lit on the family grave. The spirits of the dead are invited to join the family and then a feast is shared. Mexicans believe this friendly gesture will appease them and keep them friendly so that they will cause the family to prosper. The Tree of Life, growing from a serpent in the ground, is an ancient Mayan symbol. These trees are enormously popular in Mexico, being made in a great variety of sizes and colours.
Painted clay reinforced with wire. Height 17 ins. Traditional; still in use. Toluca and Metepec, Mexico. Author's collection.

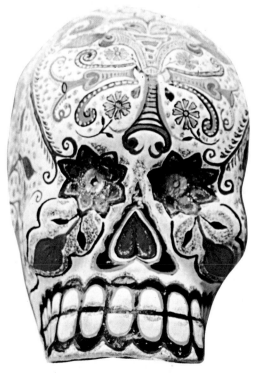

Below: Marzipan skull from Mexico, made in all sizes and sold at fiestas. Sugar skulls are made in their thousands to be sold on the Day of the Dead; to give a Mexican girl a skull is to show regard for her.
Decorated marzipan. All sizes. Traditional; still made. Mexico.

Left: This young boy is praying beside the grave of his ancestors at the Chinese spring festival of Ch'ing Ming. This day (about 5 April), known as 'sweeping the grave' day, is the public holiday in China (Hong Kong etc.) on which the living relations take food and gifts (paper 'money', etc.) to the graves of their dead. They sweep and clean the graves, share a meal and pray for the indulgence of the dead. Fire-crackers are exploded to keep away demons. Ch'ing Ming is the time for the germination of crops, so it is prudent as well as pious to engage ancestral attention, which can bring a good harvest. Formerly the children carried willow branches: willows are a rain symbol.

Traditionally followers of Confucius and worshippers of Buddha, these modern Chinese peasants from the Hungching Production Brigade, in Taitsang County, Kiangsu, are reading the thoughts of Chairman Mao in their little red books during the festivities on their collective farm to celebrate the National Congress of the Republic of China of 1969. The little red book has become a Chinese talisman. Is Chairman Mao in process of deification?

Conclusion

The daughters of Yunnan witches in south-west China, though still wearing their traditional magic-red triangular turbans with lucky tassels, are now studying Mao Tse-tung's little red book.

Outside Bombay, in the famous caves of Elephanta, Trimuri, the triple-faced Shiva, is daily worshipped, and the devout pray to the great stone *lingam*, to the androgynous Colossus leaning on a bull, and to the lotus-faced Brahma, who has four faces and five swans. Close by these caves the Indians have built a large atomic energy plant.

In the USSR the sons of superstitious peasants were the first men in outer space.

In Chinese villages, instead of their former vast wall-paintings of the Buddha, peasants today paint giant images of Chairman Mao.

Whilst the East, under the banner of Karl Marx, is rapidly becoming industrialized and staging atomic tests, there is a revulsion against industrialization in the West. This has come to a head in the universities of Europe and America, where the students have been staging protests against what they see as the hollowness of industrialized life.

The youth of the West are searching for a religion other than the Christian Church, which many of them ignore or reject. Some of them are turning to Buddhism or Hindu-ism for enlightenment. Interest in Eastern mysticism has never been keener than at present. Files of American students with shaven heads and saffron robes are a common sight in the streets of London today. Beating drums and chanting 'Hare Krishna! Hare Krishna! Krishna, Krishna! Hare Hare! Hare Rama! Hare Rama! Rama, Rama! Hare Hare!', these are followers of Swami Prabhupad, leader of the Society for Krishna Consciousness, and they believe in love, feasting, dancing and pacifism. On a different level there is the expanding Buddhist Society, founded in 1924.

The youth of Europe (especially Britain) have for some years been wearing lively mixtures of *shalwas*, caftans, prayer-robes, country smocks, talismans and amulets, praying-beads and Eastern rosaries, besides headbands and fringed suède borrowed from the Red Indians. They are paying homage to what they regard as preferable civilizations.

There is also an insatiable public for books and magazines about mysticism and magic cults, including black magic. Current advertisements in the magazine *Prediction* offer the services of clairvoyants and clairvoyantes, tarot consultants, mediums, occulists, psychometrists, Red Indian seers, palmists, specialists in magic mirrors, psychic consultants, powerful psychic inner perceptionists, intuitive advisers, Egyptian sand

A traditional pattern of life. This recent painting of his native village by a young Balinese artist reveals a world in which every act of daily life is an act of worship. The villagers are moving without haste in their traditional tasks, stopping first to pray and offer flowers at the shrines. They are weeding and planting in the irrigated paddy fields, loading and carrying food, fishing, climbing trees for fruit, chatting. And at night there will be music and the dancing of traditional epics in which they will all take part. A Bali Hilton, new airport and airline are now bringing regular tourists to Den Pasar, but traditional Balinese village life continues.
Ikisoki Ubud. Gouache on board. 40×26 ins. Modern. Bali. Mrs Patricia Sinclair collection.

readers, card readers, dice-reading experts, trance mediums, psychic healers, Welsh seers, dream interpreters, prayer group consultants, Chinese and Javanese card readers, yoga teachers, astrologers, numeralogists, teachers of premonition, monition, telepathic communication and intuitive insight, aura interpreters, arc of power professors, and spirit-guide portrait vendors.

The time comes when peasants and workers cease to hope for assistance from idols and organize themselves into unions to fight for benefits. But the political revolutions which, in this century, have overturned ancient gods and destroyed ancient magic beliefs are themselves creating new gods, new magic beliefs and new mysticisms. For people must worship something. And so today magic advances and recedes, taking new forms in the East and returning to ancient forms in the West.

Right: This 'rude' seaside picture postcard is typical of those circulated and enjoyed by English working class people on holiday. The two old ladies (though they do not know it) are concerned not only with sexual symbols but with the protection of fertility. The sacred rites of sex have become a joke. *Modern. England.*

When a society becomes
industrialized, as did
Britain in the late 18th
and 19th centuries, the
ancient symbols based on
pastoral fertility become
confused and disintegrate.
Farmhands leave the land
for crowded cities, work
in mines, forges and
factories, together with
their wives and young
children. Sunset no longer
ends the day's toil. The
old lunar holidays are
upset. The home, family
pastimes, family meals,
the very look of the sky,
are broken up and lost.
Dirt and exhaustion do
not favour popular art,
though they do breed
revolutionary songs.
In time industrial workers
learn to band together
into provident societies
and burial clubs which
later develop into trade
councils and trade unions.
Instead of praying for
help, they learn to rely
on their group strength
to demand economic
security from the new
plenty produced by their
physical efforts. In Britain
the new movement needed
symbols which the austere
chapels of an indust-
rialized society could not
supply. Though his
sympathies were with the
traditional rural way of
life, William Morris understood the workers' need
and tried to supply visual
expression of their hopes.
But his barefoot ladies
carrying torches puzzled
the industrialized workers,
who loved gay colours
and associated bare feet
not with victory but with
penury. The illustrations
from two anti-factory
pro-farming pamphlets
show the type of work he
and his school were
producing. The ceramic
popular plate celebrates
the 1912 Insurance Act,
the first breakthrough in
the fight for worker-
security.
(left and bottom right)
10×9 ins. and 8×6 ins.
1870s. England. Transport
House collection.
(top right) Ceramic.
Diameter 10 ins. Collection
of Rt. Hon. Sir F. Elwyn
Jones, QC MP.

Below: The true popular art of industrialized Britain came from the East London workshops of George Tutill, in the form of the thousands of magnificent labour banners produced in the seventy years between 1870 and 1940, when his workshops were destroyed by bombing. Every branch of every new trade union ordered one, had it painted precisely to its own wishes, saved up to buy it and was proud to carry it into action and march behind it. Some have survived two world wars and are still carried at the Durham Miners' Gala and important demonstrations. Double-sided, woven of pure silk, painted and gilded with the best paints, mounted on fine brocade, all specially prepared in the Tutill workshops, they were what the workers wanted. Enormous, handsome, and with straightforward brotherly sentiments expressed in simple pictures and gorgeous lettering, these very British banners are the first and only authentic industrial folk-art in the world.
George Tutill. Silk. 8×7 ft. 1880. London.

Right top: Today Eastern and Western artists influence each other, the East benefiting from the technical sophistication of the West, the West from the strong symbolism of Eastern art. Malcolm Goddard was so impressed by African sculpture that he began to construct figures like this metal-debris fertility symbol.
Malcolm Goddard. Broken gardening fork, eyelet, metal tubing, screw. Height 18 ins. Modern. London.

Far right top: This remarkable water-colour, by an African artist from the Congo using Western materials, is a window into the African mind, a vision of lighted animated vegetation.
'Spirits' by Zic-Oma. Water-colour. 16×13 ins. Modern. Congo, Kinshasa. Author's collection.

Right bottom: This expanding silver English-made ring is, consciously or unconsciously, a perfect echo of the Chinese *yang-yin* (male/female) spiral principle.
David Pearce. Silver. Modern. Britain. Author's collection.

Below: Whether Chairman Mao really looks like the Buddha or not 800 million Chinese so regard him. Chinese peasants like their gods to be large and stout. On every commune wall where Chairman Mao is painted the resemblance becomes more emphatic. The ancient Godhead of truth, right-iousness and correct thinking has now merged completely into the Helms-man who can be depended upon, the declarer that the East is Red (lucky colour), and the family poet who gives rural fables (like the old man and the mountain) a modern application. Moreover Buddha, how-ever he was entreated, did not stop the famines in the old days, whereas Chair-man Mao has succeeded in feeding his 800 million worshippers.

Acknowledgments

People

This book is based on examples of popular art I have collected in the last thirty years. I would like to thank friends in Africa, Australia, China, the Fiji Islands, Great Britain, India, Mexico, the USA, the USSR, and the Windward Islands for helping me. In particular: Dr Mulk Raj Anand, Arthur Blundell of the Buddhist Society, Gordon Bohlin of Ayres Rock, Dame Hilda Byroe and Peter Byroe, Hugh Cobb, Bill Dunlop, Mrs Shrila Flather, Gaston le Forestier, Robert Graves, W. Howes-Bassett of Newham Education Department, Heinz Edgar Kiewe, James Laver, Alan Lefévre, Valetta Malinowska, Hal Missingham, Maung Ohn, Hugh Paget of the British Council, John Russell of the British Embassy in Kinshasa, Mrs O'Shea and my coster friends, Miss D. M. Samiar, Dr Samson, Marie de Teliga, Dr The The, Bill Vines, Mrs Wagner of Transport House Library, Benjamin Walker and Dr Stanley Wang.

Books

Among the most helpful books I have studied were the following:

Afrique: Les Civilisations Noires by Jacques J. Macquet. Horizons de France, Paris, 1962.

Annual Customs and Festivals in Peking by Tun Li-Ch'en. Henri Vetch, Peiping, 1936.

The Art of the North-east Frontier of India by Verrier Elwin. Arthur Probsthain, London, 1959.

Ballads and Stories of Tun-huang by Arthur Waley. Allen & Unwin, London, 1960.

Black Magic in China Known as Ku by Feng Han Yee and J. K. Shylock. Thesis read in University of Hong Kong Library in 1960.

Chinese Magic and Superstitions in Malaya by Leon Comber. Donald Moore, Singapore, 1955.

Encyclopedia of Chinese Symbolism and Art Motives by C. A. S. Williams. The Julian Press, New York, 1960.

Dessins Rupestres du Bas-Congo by Paul Raemaekers and Hendrik van Moorsel. Editions de l'Université de Leopoldville, Kinshasa, 1964 (very limited edition).

Destination Chungking by Han Suyin. Jonathan Cape, London, 1953.

Divine Horsemen by Maya Deren. Thames & Hudson, London, 1953.

Foreign Mud by Maurice Collis. Faber & Faber, London, 1964.

The Forgotten Pictorial Language of Israel by Heinz Edgar Kiewe. Kiewe, Oxford, 1951.

Hindu Religion, Customs and Manners by P. Thomas. D. B. Taraporevala, Bombay, 1960 (4th edition).

The Hindu World: An Encyclopedic Survey of Hinduism by Benjamin Walker. Allen & Unwin, London, 1968.

Indian Sign Language by William Tomkins. Dover Publications, London, 1969.

Journey Among Men by Jock Marshall and R. Drysdale. Hodder & Stoughton, London, 1962.

The Land of the Great Image by Maurice Collis. Faber & Faber, London, 1953 (2nd edition).

Migration of Symbols by Donald A. Mackenzie. Kegan Paul, London, 1926.

Moko or Maori Tattooing by Major-General Robley. Chapman & Hall, London, 1896.

With Mystics and Magicians in Tibet by Alexandra David-Neel. John Lane, London, 1931.

The Passing of the Aborigines by Daisy Bates. John Murray, London, 1966.

People of the Potlach by Audrey Hawthorn. University of British Columbia, Vancouver, 1956.

Pierced Hearts and True Love by Hans Ebensten. Verschoyle, London, 1953.

La Vie Quotidienne des Azteques by Jacques Soustelle. Hachette, Paris, 1959.

Wanderings in China by C. F. Gordon Cumming. Blackwood, London, 1886.

Photographs

Acknowledgment is given to the following publishers: The Julian Press, Inc., and their book *Encyclopaedia of Chinese Symbolism and Art Motives* by C. A. S. Williams (1960), for the left-hand illustration on page 16; Alfred A. Knopf, Inc., and their book *Indian Art of Mexico and Central America* by Miguel Covarrubias (1957), for the upper illustration on page 35; S.P.C.K. and Morehouse-Barlow Co., Inc., and the book *Saints, Signs and Symbols* by W. Ellwood Post (1964), for the illustration on page 12; Thames & Hudson Ltd., and their book *Divine Horsemen* by Maya Deren, for the right-hand illustration on page 109; *The Times of Ceylon Annual 1963* for the left-hand illustration on page 61. The lower illustration on page 119 is reproduced by kind permission of Bamforth & Co. Ltd., Holmfirth, Yorkshire.

Publishers

Author's collection and line drawings 17 left, 21, 43 right, 60 bottom right, 69 bottom right, 90 left, 114 bottom right
BPC Publishing Ltd 28–29, 98 bottom
Camera Press 30–31, 72–73
J. Allan Cash 99 top
Central Press Photos 116–117
Hugh Cobb 114 bottom left
Douglas Dickens 38, 50
Kerry Dundas 26 right, 28 right, 76 bottom, 90 bottom, 118–119
Les Graves 18–19
Hawkley Studio Associates Ltd front jacket right and bottom left, back jacket, 1, 10, 16 right, 22 top, 24–25 top, 25, 27 bottom, 42, 43 left, 44 bottom, 45, 46 top, 48, 49, 52 bottom, 56, 57, 58–59, 60 top, 60 bottom left, 61, 62, 63, 64, 67 top right, 68 bottom, 69 centre left, 69 bottom left, 77, 81 bottom left, 82, 83, 84, 85 top, 88 top left, 88 bottom, 89, 92 top left, 92 top right, 93 bottom, 96 top, 103, 105, 110 top, 111, 113 top, 115 top, 120, 121, 122, 123 top, 123 bottom left
Hong Kong Government Information Office 115 bottom left
Kristina Jardel 46 bottom, 47 left
Keystone Press Agency 6–7, 114 top
S. L. Lewis front jacket, 9, 13, 14, 15, 16 left, 16 bottom, 17 bottom, 22 bottom, 23, 24, 26 left, 27 top, 32, 35 bottom left, 35 bottom right, 40 left, 41, 44 top, 52 top, 54, 55 right, 66, 67 top left, 67 bottom, 68 top, 69 top left, 70 top, 71, 75, 76 top, 78, 80, 81 top, 85 centre left, 85 bottom left, 85 bottom right, 86, 87 top, 88 top right, 91, 92 bottom, 93 top, 93 left, 94, 95 top left, 95 top right, 95 bottom left, 96 bottom, 97 top left, 97 bottom, 98 top, 99 centre left, 99 centre right, 106, 107, 110 right, 112, 123 left
John Player & Sons 93 bottom
Popperfoto 37, 100–101
Portrait of Mexico Exhibition 28 left, 87 bottom
Marc Riboud Magnum Photos 39
Scott & Browne Ltd 17 right
Snark International 115 bottom right
The Society for Promoting Christian Knowledge (copyright © 1962 by Morehouse-Barlow Co.) 12
Sunday Telegraph 123 bottom right
Warwickshire Photographic Survey 90 top

Index

The figures in bold type refer to illustrations.

Adam and Eve (painting) **88**
African divination ritual **44**
African initiation dance **72**
After-life, image of 102–6, **113**
Agwe, god of the sea (Haiti) **109**
Algonquin fertility dance (J. White) **29**
Amahs (housemaids), deity protecting Chinese **42**
Amarnath, Cave of **30**
Angel, marble, in English cemetery **15**
Angus, Peggy **24**, **110**
Animism **79**, **97**
Ara, insignia of (Australian) **47**
Avizan, goddess of spirit protection (Haiti) **109**
Aztec clay playthings **90**

Baby-sling (Chinese) **89**
Balinese
    corn dolly **82**
    dance-mask **91**
    village life **119**
Bates, Daisy **103**
Bee-hive devil mask **97**
Béjar, Feliciano **28**, **87**
Birrahgnooloo, goddess of water (aborigine) **34**
Black magic 23, 79–80
Bocor, female demon (Haiti) **103**
Bodhisattva, head of **99**
Boy's initiation rites
    aborigine **75**
    at public school **74**
Boy with sunflower (carved) **85**
Braguette (codpiece) **52**
Brahmin caste marks 11
Buddha **38**
    carved into rock-face (Afghanistan) **37**
    ear-lobes of 9
    female **43**
    gold image of **36**
    head of **39**
    Mao compared to **123**
    painting of in Lamaist tradition **32**
    powers of 34
Buddhist Society **118**
Burial rites **100**, 102–8

Calyste, Canute **80**, **110**
Candle, vegetable-shaped Mexican wax **23**
Carrying-ring with mirrors (Indian) **94**
Cave drawings, stone-age (Lovo) **18–19**, **87**
Ceiling with protective motifs (Australian) **69**
Ceramic tile, modern (P. Angus) **24**, **110**
Chandelier, resurrection (Polish) **112**
Charms, demon-repellent **16**, 79
    wooden (Polish) **93**
Chest with demon-repellent design (Slovakia) **70**
Childbirth protecting figures (East Indies) **86**
Children
    and initiation rites **74**, **75**
    death sentence for **114**
    magical protection of 74, 102
    preference and protection of boys in primitive cultures 74, **85**, **90**
Chinese poster, modern **32**
Ch'ing Ming festival **105**, **115**
'Chrising Paty' (C. Calyste) West Indian painting **80**
Christian angel, used as demon-repellent **103**
Cigarette cards with ship figureheads **93**
Cigar-holder **63**
Clock tower with protective figures (Brighton) **61**
Cock, symbol of male virility **85**
Coconut birds (Indian carving) **85**
Colours, magic significance of **16**, 53, 78, **96**, **116**, 118, **123**
Concentration camp, Germany **114**
Corn dolly
    19th century **24**
    Balinese **82**
    from the Balkans **83**
Coster kings, London's **46**, **47**
Cowrie shells, symbols of fertility **94**
Crochet and embroidery designs (Polish) **65**

Cross
    as a symbol of Christianity **10**, 11–12, **12**
    other symbolic interpretations of 23

Dana, Richard Henry 102
Dance-mask **17**
    Balinese **91**
    Congolese **91**
    from Ceylon **42**
    from Orissa **91**
    modern Bolivian **92**
    New Guinea fertility **90**
    of Shiva **98**
    of the Kwakiutl tribe **106**
Day of the Dead (Mexico) **106**, **115**
Dead, appeasement of 102–6
Decapitation, practices of 103
Demon-scarer **16**, **103**
de Nobili, Robert 11
Devil-mask
    for a bee-hive **97**
Diabolo sign **87**
Disease mask **17**
'Disturbance in Heaven' (Peking opera) **43**
Dola-yātrā ceremony 24
Dragon-boat race (Hong Kong) **33**
Dragon, mystical animal of China 10, 20, **32**, **33**, **34**
Dudgeon, Dr **36**

Easter biscuits (Polish) **77**
Effigies of British sovereigns **48**
Egg decoration (Polish) **112**
El Alamein fountain **28**
Elephant, toy **95**
Eliot, George 102
Elizabeth II, Queen of England 10
Erzulie, goddess of love (Haiti) **109**
Eskimo carving **76**
Evil Eye (image) 11
    magic power of 78–9, **98**, **99**
Evil spirit mask (by Dan Jones) **92**
Evil spirits
    appeasement of 53, 102–8
    listed on Chinese print **96**
Execution rituals 103
'Eye-bestowal' rite (Hindu) **99**
Eye, magic and third 78–9, **98**, **99**
Eye of God, Jewish pattern **10**
Eye of Horus **98**
Eye or *Urna* of Bodhisattva **99**

Fan, ceremonial Nigerian **52**
Fatimah, magic-protective hand of 78, **99**
Feng-shui, magic power 104–5
Fertility
    and childbirth 74
    mask **91**
    symbols **17**, **18–19**, 20–4, **22**, **24**, **26**, 77, **80**, **85**, **119**
    symbols in modern Britain **120**
Fetishism 10
Fisherwoman from Mexico (straw) **78**
Fishing boat with eyes (Portuguese) **99**
Fish sign, Tunisian **93**
'Flying Dragon Dancing Phoenix' (Chinese poster) **32**
Foliate paper man from Mexico **81**
Food, magic and protection of 63, 76–8, **97**
Fork and spoon, Indian **62**
Fortune-sticks **36**
French, Leonard **20**
Freud, Sigmund 36
Funeral
    bier from Singapore **114**
    procession **110**
    rites 102–8

Ganesh, god of fortune (India) 33–4, **95**
Garuda, mythical Hindu deity **41**
Ghede, guardian god of the dead (Haiti) **109**
Gill, Madge **109**, **113**
Giranta insignia (aborigine) **90**
Goat-head mask **86**
Goat of straw, used for sympathetic magic (Sweden) **76**
Goddard, Malcolm **123**
Gods
    bringing security 36
    importance of their power 33–6
Good spirit mask (by Dan Jones) **92**
Grandville **111**
Gravepost, Vietnamese **112**

Graves, Robert 10
Green Man (spirit of germination) **81**
Gregory XV, Pope 10–11

Haircomb, shaped like an elephant (Indian) **95**
Haiti tattoo **55**
Hallowe'en festival **106**
Hand of Fatimah 78, **99**
Hanuman, Hindu monkey deity 34, **40**, **43**
Harriet, gypsy queen **100**
Hindu festival 23
Hindu funeral ceremony 102
Hindu kolems **61**, **105**
Hindu pilgrims **30**
Home, magic powers to protect the 53–4, **62**, **66**, **69**, **97**, **105**
Hook, carved by Iatmul tribe **26**
Hookah **63**
Horses as guardian figures **66**
Horses, clay guardian (Bengal) **67**
Horus, Eye of **98**
Hou Hao **105**
Hunting club (aborigine) **108**
Hunting trophies 75–6

Iatmul tribe, hook used by **26**
Igbava (Nigerian custom) **104**
Imagery 10–11
    see also Symbols
Indian bedcover, with border **64**
Indian fork and spoon **62**
Industrial folk-art, British **122**
Initiation rites and practices **72**, 74–5, **75**, **90**
Isaac, Sacrifice of (Muslim drawing) **13**
Ixcuintle (Mexican hairless dog) **49**

Jagarnath, chariot of Orissa **22**
Jamalagni, sage **40**
Jehovah 10, 20
Jewel-box, owl-shaped **70**
Jewellery, as magic protection **50**, **52**, **54**, **57**, 78, **81**, 104, **123**
Jews
    and early symbols 10
    interpretation of the triangle 10
Jones, Dan **88**, **92**
Jug, symbol of the female (Mexican) **86**

Kaidiche, executioner's slippers (aborigine) **114**
Kali, goddess 23
Kartavirya, King **40**
Kasyapa, Hindu sage **40**
Kenyatta, President of Kenya **52**
Kirke, Percy 131
Kitchen spoon and stirrer (Angola) **63**
Kites, magic significance of **84**
Kohl, Arab magic protective 52
Kolem, Hindu **61**, **105**
Kookaburra **69**
Krishna, god of love 23, 34
    birth of (toy model) **88**
    clay figure of **32**
    statue of **35**
Krishna Consciousness, Society of **118**
Kuan Yin, Chinese goddess of mercy **43**
Ku witches and magic 79–80
Kwakiutl tribe (Canada)
    dance mask of **106**

Lanka of *Ramayana* **42**
Laver, James 23
Lincoln's Inn gate **58**
Lingam (ancient symbol of transmission of life) 23, 118
Lions, protective ceramic (Chinese) **67**
Loa, voodoo spirit **106**, **109**
Lombardi Indian gypsy woman **50**
Lovo caves (Congo) **18–19**, **18**, **87**
Luna Park gate **60**

MacNamara 8
Magic power and symbols 8–10, 53
    basic aim of 8
    black 23, 79–80
    defined 8–10
    importance of sex regarding 11–12
    in foods and medicine 76–8
    of *Ku* 79–80

agic protection/protective
borders 10, **17**, **25**, 52, **56**,
64, **68**, **69**, **94**
during burial rites 102–8
fertility dance mask **90**
Mexican cut-paper flags **11**
of family and livelihood 62,
74–80
of the body and dwelling 52–4,
61, **62**, **66**, **68**, **69**, **97**, **105**
on doorways 20, 22, **22**, **58**, 105
papercuts **10**, **60**, **108**
Magiscopios' (F. Béjar) **28**
Malaya tattoo chart 55
Mantras (funeral ritual) 102
Maori
moko (tattooing) **22**
Mao Tse-tung 33
little red books of **116**, 118, **123**
Marriage contracts and
protection of 74
Marshall, Professor Jock 33
Marx, Karl 118
Masks see Dance-masks
Mat from Domenica **27**, **112**
Maya, mother of Buddha **95**
Maypole dance, English 24
Medals, symbolism and use of 75–6
Medicine, magic of 76–7
Mexican queen, image of **49**
Mexican shift with motifs **17**
Mexican straw angels **14**
Mezuzzah (talismanic case) **60**
Miaou tribal magic-protective
sleeve borders **56**
Mirrors, demon-repellent 52, **52**, 54,
54, **94**
animated (by M. Oved) **97**
sun-rayed Mexican **68**
Mohammed, Prophet 78, **93**, **99**
Moldavian rug **64**
Money-box, magically protected **71**
Monkey, magic deity (China) 34, 36
Montespan, Madame de 80
Moon Festival (Chinese) 23
Moon symbol 22–3
Morris, William **120**, **121**
Movement as a magic generating
power 23, **29**
Muslim prints of 'graven images' **13**
Myrninerest (spirit) **109**

Naga Kadru (wife of Kasyapa) **40**
Nasser, President of Egypt funeral
ceremony of 102
Necklace, Polynesian shell and
seed **81**

Obeah witchcraft 80
Orifices, magic protection of 52–3
Oved, Mosheh **97**

Pamphlets and banners,
modern English **120**, **121**, **122**
Papercuts, as magic protection
10, **60**, **81**, **108**
Parasurama (sixth incarnation of
Vishnu) **40**
Peace/Life (Picasso) **9**
Pearly kings and queens 46, **47**
Percy, George 22
Picasso, Pablo **9**
Pillow, cat-shaped (Chinese) 53, **71**
Plate, Polish with fertility patterns
68, **69**
Polo, Marco 104
Postcard, English seaside **119**

'Rainbow Serpent' (L. French) **21**
Rain gods 33–4
Rain symbols and use of 20, **20**, 23
Rama (seventh incarnation of
Vishnu) **40**
Ramayana **40**
Ravana, Hindu demon king 34, **40**
Red Kangaroo tribe (Australian) **47**
Reincarnation, belief in 102
Religion and magic 10–12
Rice bowl with moon pattern
(Chinese) **69**
Ring, modern English **123**
Ring with mirror (Indian) **52**
Rod
symbol of phallic power 23
used by women 23

Sacrifices **13**, 80, 106
Sardanyas (circular sun-dance) 24
Savu Savu (Tapa painting) **25**
Sewing machine with protective
gold border **94**

Sex, importance of in the context of
magic 11–12, **87**
Shakkas 106
Shamans **17**, 80, **105**
Shango, god of thunder 36
deity of the west coast of
Africa 33
West Indian deity 33
Shapiro, Haim Moshe 74
Sheba, Queen of **89**
Shemah Israel (Jewish prayer) 60
Ship in light bulb **46**
Shiva, Hindu god 23, **30**, 34, 77, 118
dance-mask of **98**
statue of **35**
third eye of 79, **99**
Shrine, primitive metal **85**
Signature drawing (vévé) **109**
Sioux sign-writing **110**
Sita **40**
Skull, marzipan (Mexican) **115**
Smith, John 22, 36
Solomon, King 20, **89**
So-menpo or iron faceguard
(Japanese) **91**
Spaniels, Welsh (ceramic) **66**
Spiral (fertility or rain symbol) 20,
22, **23**, **123**
'Spirits' Zic-Oma (African artist) **123**
Spirits
conjuring up of 106–7, passim
fire (aborigine) **104**
trap (Tibetan) **105**
Spirit-writing **109**, **110**
Star of David, sacred 10
Sun symbols **18–19**, **26**, **27**, **28**, **68**
and dances 24
use of by various cultures 20–2
Sun (Sioux) fertility symbol **18–19**
Sun Wu Kung, Chinese monkey
deity **43**
Supernatural terror,
drawing (Grandville) **111**
Swallow kite **84**
Swami Prabhupad 118
Swan, symbol of resurrection
(European) **113**
Swastika, symbol of movement
18–19, 23–4
Symbols
of common people 10, **70**
of fertility 20–4
use and understanding of
8–10, passim

Tantric cults 23
Taoist good luck charm **16**
Tapa painting (headman of Savu
Savu) **25**
Tattoo **18**, **22**, 55, **55**, 76
Teapot, mother and child
(English) **69**
Telekowska, Professor Wanda **68**
Te Pehi Kupe, Maori Chief
mask of **22**
Thor, god of thunder 33
Tibetan Buddha, painting of **32**
Tlaloc, rain god (Aztec) 34, **35**
Tools, magic powers of **62**, **63**, 79,
97
Toothpick holder **62**
Totemism **106**
Toys
as magical symbols **75**, **88**
Mexican demon-repellent **90**
Tree of life
Mexican **115**
Polish papercut **10**, **60**
Trivits **27**
Trophies, symbolism of 75–6
Tunisian tattoo patterns **55**
Turon with goat-head mask
(Polish) **86**
Tutill, George **122**

Urna or eye of Bodhisattva **99**

Vegetable cutter, in animal form **97**
Vegetable pounder, diabolo shape
(African) **87**
Victorian glass vase **71**
Vévé (voodoo drawing) 106, **109**
Victoria, Queen of England
48, 61
Victory, carved image of **48**
Vinyata (wife of Kasyapa) **40**
Vishnu, Hindu god 34, **35**, 67
incarnations of **40**
Voodoo, religion of Haiti 106, 107,
109

Waninga (aborigine insignia) **47**

War/Death (Picasso) **9**
Wat Chayamangkalaram (reclining
Buddha) **38**
White, John 29
Witch coven, insignia of **87**
Woodcut from Vietnam **80**

Yama, god of death (Chinese) 106
Yasodhara, wife of Buddha 34
Yemaya, goddess of moisture
(African) 33
Yunnan witches (Chinese) 118
Yupa ceremony 24

'Zombies' (powerless spirits) 103